Charles Sylvain

Spiritual Direction for the Use of Religious Communities

Charles Sylvain

Spiritual Direction for the Use of Religious Communities

ISBN/EAN: 9783337428280

Printed in Europe, USA, Canada, Australia, Japan

Cover: Foto ©Lupo / pixelio.de

More available books at **www.hansebooks.com**

FOR THE USE OF

RELIGIOUS COMMUNITIES.

By the Author of "Golden Sands."

TRANSLATED FROM THE FRENCH BY

Miss ELLA McMAHON.

New York, Cincinnati, and St. Louis:
BENZIGER BROTHERS,
PRINTERS TO THE HOLY APOSTOLIC SEE

1884.

Imprimatur,

JOHN, CARDINAL McCLOSKEY,

Archbishop of New York.

COPYRIGHT, 1884, BY BENZIGER BROTHERS.

Approbations.

FROM MGR. DUBREIL, ARCHBISHOP OF AVIGNON.

The work bearing the title *Spiritual Direction* has been examined by our Commission. Upon the favorable report given us, we authorize the printing of it and we recommend it be read by the religious Communities of our Diocese for whom it is written.

† LOUIS,
Archbishop of Avignon.
Avignon, September 25, 1873.

FROM MGR. GONIN, ARCHBISHOP OF PORT OF SPAIN.

GENTLEMEN :
I have had the pleasure of receiving the copy of the Treatise, *Spiritual Direction* which you kindly sent to me.
It suffices to consider the precious sources whence the writer has drawn, I mean the Saints and Doctors, to be convinced that this publication cannot but be very salutary to pious souls for whom it is principally destined.

† FR. JOACHIM LOUIS,
Archbishop of Port of Spain.
Trinidad, January 8, 1874.

FROM MGR. FORCADE, ARCHBISHOP OF AIX.

. . . .
The correctness of doctrine and the spirit of wisdom manifest in the editing of the book, persuade us to recommend it very particularly to the religious Communities of our diocese.

† AUGUSTINE,
Archbishop of Aix.
Aix, February 24, 1874.

From Mgr. Mermillod, Bishop of Hebron,
Vicar-Apostolic of Geneva.

Gentlemen:

You are untiring servants of the truth. You are about to publish now a small work on *Spiritual Direction* which merits our best approval. These pages will be useful to souls in learning the secrets of Christian perfection.

† Gaspard,
Bishop of Hebron,
Vicar-Apostolic of Geneva.

Fernex, Nov. 4, 1875.
Feast of St. Charles.

From Mgr. Robert, Bishop of Constantine and of Hippone.

Gentlemen :

. . . . There are yet, thank God, a great number of souls called to practice the perfection of Evangelical Counsels, in the religious state. These privileged souls are like the divine salt which prevents corruption from spreading on the earth. But in the sublime path which they are following, they are exposed to dangerous illusions, unless they meet with a sure guide for their conduct. The little book which you have published, shows them in a clear and precise manner, how they should practice the "Direction" which is so important for advancement in perfection. I believe it will effect much good throughout the religious Communities.

† Louis,
Bishop of Constantine and of Hippone.

Constantine, December 1, 1875.

Approbations. 5

FROM MGR. GROLLEAU, BISHOP OF EVREAUX.

. . . . . This book, written clearly and with unction, shows the author to be one of wise experience in the conduct of souls. We willingly add Our approbation to that of Our Venerable colleagues, in favor of this work.

† FRANCIS,
Bishop of Evreaux.
Evreaux, December 15, 1873.

FROM MGR. BECEL, BISHOP OF VANNES.

GENTLEMEN:
I will recommend to the religious communities of my diocese, the little work entitled *Spiritual Direction*. They will find in it wise counsels. May my humble commendation please the pious writer, and contribute to the success of his works.

† JEAN-MARIE,
Vannes, December 16, 1875. Bishop of Vannes.

FROM MGR. MABILE, BISHOP OF VERSAILLES.

By order of Mgr. the Bishop of Versailles, I have read the little work entitled "Spiritual Direction for the use of religious communities."
This work appears to me to contain correct doctrine, substantial and of a nature to keep up the spirit of piety in the communities for which it is destined.
The Canon-Dean of the Chapter.
BORMAND, Char.V.G.

Having read the report of M. the Dean of the Chapter, We approve this little work.
† PIERRE,
Bishop of Versailles.
Versailles, December 23, 1873.

PREFACE.

I.

"Obedience," says St. Augustine, "is the fiery chariot into which the Prophet Elias entered and in which he was swiftly borne to heaven. Happy the souls who enter this chariot with no other thought than to continue in it and allow themselves to be borne upward."

After all, what matters a more or less commodious position?

What matter more or less violent shocks since we know we are on the route that each moment brings us nearer the goal, and that the guide whatever his exterior bearing, language, manner of speaking, is himself guided by the spirit of God?

Our only care must be not to abandon the chariot which is bearing us on to the goal.

II.

The road of obedience is *sure*, but sometimes *difficult :* and in the road to Heaven as in every other, the sun parches and burns us, the dust stifles us, we are bruised by the stones, and pierced by the thorns. There are times during the journey when everything seems lost. Clouds envelope the chariot; it experiences rude shocks, the guide himself seems to us astray, and discouraged and frightened we would turn from the path.

God foresaw all these discouraging trials, and to alleviate them He has placed along the route shelters in which we may rest, springs at which we may be refreshed. God foresaw all these discouraging trials, and to alleviate them He has willed that the guide in charge of the chariot should be *Guide and Father* in one.

As Guide, he causes it to move, and impels it forward. As Father, he loves us, consoles us, encourages us.

III.

The object of this work useful to all pious souls though intended principally for religious communities, is to set forth the mission of *Guide* and *Father* which God has confided to Superiors.

The sentiments of a father are never absent from the heart of a superior, but they are particularly manifested in those hours of converse which, under the name of *direction*, draw to his own heart the hearts of those who submit themselves to him.

Ah! would we might make *direction* known and loved. How the *trials* of the religious life would then be sweetened ! Doubtless they would not cease, for they enter into God's designs for our sanctification, but with what resignation they would be borne and how meritorious they would be !

IV.

All that we have said is gathered from the writings of Saints and Doctors of the Church. The works of Tronson, the Mystical Theology of Schram, the Ascetic Guide by Scaramelli, *Le petit traité sur la direction, par* Mgr. Rey, Bishop of Annecy—the works of P. Surin, of P. Grou, of P. St. Jure, of St. Francis de Sales, the different treatises of Rodriguez, and various ascetic works, all approved by the Church, have served us as guide and furnished the most beautiful pages of our book.

Therefore we offer it with confidence to pious souls, humbly asking a few prayers from those whose hearts we shall have expanded.

CONTENTS.

PREFACE.. 7
DEFINITION OF SPIRITUAL DIRECTION........ 15

CHAPTER I.—*Necessity of a Director.*

1st. For persons called to perfection........... 22
    Proofs furnished by authority............ 22
    Proofs furnished by reason............... 28
        From the nature of a perfect life.... 28
        From obstacles encountered in this life.. 28
        From illusions encountered in this life.. 30
        From the maladies incident to this life.. 32
2d. For all states and conditions............. 36
3d. For all times and seasons................. 41
4th. For all kinds of actions.................. 41

CHAPTER II.—*Advantages of Direction.*

1st. For communities............................ 44
2d. For individuals:
    It opens the heart........................ 48
    It dilates the heart...................... 49
    It gives peace............................ 50
    It causes one to advance in virtue.. 53
    It causes one to taste the joys of holy friendship................................ 55

CHAPTER III.—*Choice of a Director.*

An appointed Director............................ 61
Freedom in the choice of a Director............ 71
Prayer to ask of God a Director................. 85

Chapter IV.—*Abuse of Direction.*

1st. A multiplicity of Directors 86
2d. Changing Directors 90
3d. Relations with a Director:
    Attachment for a Director 96
    Dislike for a Director 101
    Reserve with a Director 104

Chapter V.—*Duties of the soul directed.*

1st. To pray much for her Director 112
2d. To seriously will to become better 114
3d. To be simple 115
4th. To be obedient 118
5th. To be discreet 123
6th. To be humble 126
7th. Summary 130
8th. A few counsels 132

Chapter VI.—*Objections to Direction.*

1st. Sources of these objections 134
2d. Answers to the principal objections:
    My Director is not a priest 136
    My Director is not a saint 137
    My Director is too young 138
    I find nothing to say 139
    I cannot open my heart 140
    My Director is not discreet 141
    My Director says nothing to me, or continually reproaches me 144
    I am dissatisfied after receiving direction 146
    I prefer to seek my direction in writing 150
    I fear to weary my Director 151

Contents.

Chapter VII.—*Matter of Direction.*

1st. General principles on the matter of direction... 153
2d. Subjects which may serve as matter of direction:
    A virtue to be acquired........................... 161
    Actions 163
    Temptations....................................... 164
    Trials.. 167
    Inclinations and disposition 169
        Of the body..................................... 170
        Of the soul...................................... 171
        Of the mind 173
        Daily Life....................................... 174
        General formula 176

Chapter VIII.—*Particular counsels for Direction.*

1st. Character of pious persons................. 186
2d. Different states of pious persons.......... 190
3d. How pious persons should bear themselves in these different states........ 193
4th. Rules for discerning the spirit of God.... 195

Chapter IX.—*Practice of Direction.*

1st. *Direction:* On humility 201
2d. *Direction:* Counsels on piety................ 213
3d. *Direction:* On laxness.......................... 216

Conclusion.—*Doctrine of St. Liguori.*

1st. On the general necessity of direction..... 222
2d. On the particular necessity of direction for scrupulous souls................... 223
3d. On obedience to one's Confessor........ 233

APPENDIX.

Two Letters of Marie Lataste.

1st. Letter : Necessity of a Director............ 235
2d. Letter : How we should act towards a Director 241
Letter of St. Ignatius on Obedience.. 245

PRELIMINARY CHAPTER.

DEFINITION — NATURE — DIVISION OF THE TREATISE.

I.

Definition and Nature of Spiritual Direction.

Spiritual direction means "a summary of the counsels which a person, experienced in the ways of God and the science of the Saints, gives to a soul which asks for them in order to advance in perfection."

Observations upon the words of the definition.

We say 1st, a *summary of the counsels*, for an occasional counsel or decision does not constitute spiritual direction. Direction is a series of counsels, teachings, encouragements which, while allowing the soul perfect freedom to act for herself, never leaves her alone. A director is a *guide*, and a guide not only shows the way but accompanies us the length of the route.

2d, *An experienced person:* such a person may be a confessor, a superior a layman, or even a friend ; but he must always have the *experience* afforded by age, study, practical life, and the authority which his position or his well known devotion gives him.

3d, *A soul which asks counsel:* Direction not being, as we shall show later, of rigid precept, a soul that wishes to be guided must *ask* for direction, or *voluntarily submit* in her community, to all that the rule prescribes concerning direction.

4th, *In order to advance in perfection:* The end of direction is particularly, perfection.

We have not here to examine how far every Christian is bound to perfection by these positive words of Jesus Christ : "Be you perfect as also your heavenly Father is perfect." "Thou shalt love the Lord thy God with thy whole heart, with thy whole soul, and with all thy strength;" but all admit as certain, that persons living in a community and taking religious vows, are obliged to tend to perfection, and that direction, as we are about to explain, is a great means of attaining thereto.

Though our work may be useful to all Christians, we are writing it particularly for persons consecrated to God.

II.
Division of the Treatise.

1. Necessity of Direction.
2. Advantages of Direction.
3. Choice of Director.
4. Abuse of Direction.
5. Duties of the soul Directed.
6. Objections to Direction.
7. Matter of Direction.
8. Particular counsels on Direction.
9. Practice of Direction.

CHAPTER FIRST.

Necessity of Direction.

Direction, as we have defined it, may be independent of confession,* and as in some communities it is given by other than a confessor, it is not *absolutely necessary for salvation*.

The counsels of a confessor,—religious instructions,—spiritual books, generally indicate sufficiently the means to avoid sin and obtain salvation.

But we can say without exaggeration, that except in particular and very rare cases, direction is necessary to attain the perfection which the religious state requires.

It is the doctrine of the founders of all Orders who in their constitutions have prescribed the obligation of *spiritual direction*.

It is the thought of the Church which has approved these constitutions.

It is the teaching of the Doctors who say

---

* The direct end of confession is to purify the soul from its sins. The direct end of direction is to make it advance in virtue, by indicating the means of overcoming faults and natural inclinations which might lead it to sin.

that God, though able to guide souls by His inspirations alone, has, nevertheless, not willed to do so, and has always made use of men to form men, either to punish our disobedience and overcome our pride, or because His fatherly condescension chooses this means as better suited to our infirmity, or as St. Augustine says, because He designed to thus maintain the tie which should exist between men.

It is, finally, the practice of the Saints, all of whom regard the happiness of being under obedience to a director as an important grace, and have manifested towards him a filial and complete submission which, to us, is truly astonishing. "All have been led in this way," says St. Dorothy, "and if," adds Tronson, "God has sometimes dispensed a few from it, it has only been in rare cases; nor are we aware that He has ever done it without verifying the dispensations with many miracles and wonders, and He has thus dispensed souls, only when there was no one at hand to direct them. Therefore, though the miracles performed by a person were to equal the number of his actions, his sanctity would be doubtful if, being able to have a director, he did not submit to his guidance."

"It may happen," says Schram, "by an extraordinary providence, or, in default of a suitable person to guide the soul, or simply because God wishes to grant this singular grace, it may happen that He will deign to guide and direct her in a more sublime way Himself or by means of an angel. For God only confines Himself to His laws with the right of infringing them, if it be His greater pleasure, when an intermediary is lacking, or He wills to act miraculously."

St. Gregory, who makes the same remark, cites several examples of persons who, having no *spiritual master to ostensibly direct them*, have had God alone for their director. "But," adds the same Saint, "these are extraordinary cases and should not be cited as the rule, lest certain souls, pretending to be interiorly directed by the Holy Ghost, may cease to consider themselves disciples and aspire to be guides."

"If a person, desirous to advance in virtue, lives where a director, capable of directing him in the way of perfection, cannot be had, I have no doubt," says Scaramelli, "that God will become the spiritual master of this soul and will give him counsels and interior lights to guide him in the true way and to cause him to attain perfection, for the isolated soul, on his part, will implore this assistance from the divine Mercy, and God is in one sense obliged to supply the deficiency of His ministers. *

"If later, however, this soul, so eager to advance in perfection, finds himself where there are priests, confessors, directors, from whom he may seek counsel for the regulation of his interior and exterior actions, and if, pretending that God has become his sole and special guide, he refuse to accept the direction of His ministers, and claiming that God himself speaks to his heart, he refuse to hear the words of experienced masters to whom he may have access, he acts with great temerity and deserves that God should refuse to guide him, and Scaramelli even adds that this temerity should be punished by abandonment on the part of God, who permits him to fall into grave faults."

---

* Witness St. Honore, an example cited by St. Gregory ; he was born in the country, grew up in the society of herdsmen, and had no spiritual master who could teach him the rules of perfection.

Moses is another example ; God himself told him what he was to do, for, being in a desert, he had no one of whom to ask counsel.

Samuel, like Moses, heard God's voice, but because Samuel dwelt in the temple, the abode of the high priest Heli, from whom he could seek counsel, God sent him to the latter. God willed, says Cassian, that Samuel should be an example of deference and submission, for all those who seek from spiritual superiors rules of conduct.

⁎

In addition to these general considerations, here is something more precise.

I.

A director is generally necessary for all persons whom God calls to perfection.

In our blindness, infirmity, and misery, it is very difficult for us to attain perfection, or for the majority of Christians to attain salvation without a Director.*

Proofs furnished by authority.

"It is better that two should be together, than one;" says the Holy Spirit, "for they have the advantage of their society. If one fall, he shall be supported by the other; woe to him that is alone, for when he falleth, he hath none to lift him up. And if a man prevail against one, two shall withstand him; a threefold cord is not easily broken."—Eccles., iv. 9, 10, 12.

"Does it not seem" writes the Bishop of

---

* Some of the words of the Saints and Doctors which we are about to quote, may at first seem exaggerated; they would perhaps be exaggerations were they applied indiscriminately to all the faithful but here they only refer, as we have said, to souls called to perfection, and obliged to aspire thereto by the state which they have embraced; these souls cannot be saved without having acquired a certain *degree of perfection* which God requires of each one, and which is only known to Him.

Necessity of Direction.

Angers, "as if you read in these words the history of the incessant struggles of the interior life and the falls which we sometimes experience therein? But do you not also see by the side of the evil, that which will correct it: side by side with frailty, that which will convert it into strength? Therefore it is a principle of the religious life that we must seek from superiors direction for our own conduct, and, there is no religious community where it is not held an important duty."

"Lean not upon thy own prudence'" says the Holy Spirit: *ne innitaris prudentiæ tuæ.* —Prov. iii.5.

"Be not wise in thy own conceit: *ne sis sapiens apud te ipsum.*—Prov. iii, 7.

"Counsel shall keep thee and prudence shall preserve thee." *Consilium custodiet te et prudentia servabit te.*—Prov. ii, 11.

"Be not your own master," says St. Jerome, "and do not venture without a guide in a way which is not known to you." *

"Salvation is a *difficult science*, we must therefore have a master to instruct us in it." —St. Dorothy. †

---

* *Nec ipse te doceas, nec sine doctore ingrediaris viam quam nunquam ingressus es.*—St.
† *Opus est nobis auxilio præter ipsum Deum ; opus est aliquo etiam qui nos moderetur et gubernet.—*

"It is the most dangerous navigation; we must therefore have a pilot to direct us."—St. Basil. *

"It is a most intricate path, therefore we need a guide to lead us and save us from wandering." †

In a word, a director is absolutely necessary. "Without one," says St. Dorothy, "there is no salvation;"—"without one," says St. Vincent Ferrer, "do not expect that God will give you His grace."‡

"Without one," says Cassian, "do not expect that God will make known to you the way of perfection." §

"I have never known a person retired from the world, to be lost in any other way than by neglecting to take the advice of a director, and trusting to his own guidance. Many even affirm that there is no other

---

* *Consilii expers similis est navigio rectore carenti.—*

† *Sicut cæcus sine ductore, sic homo sine doctore rectam viam vix graditur.—*St. Augustine. *Si hi qui sunt ignari locorum, cum solertibus viarum iter adoriri gestiunt; quanto magis adolescentes cum senibus debent novum sibi iter aggredi quominus errare possint et a vero tramite virtutis deflectere.—*St. Ambrose.

‡ *Deus nunquam suam gratiam ministrabit alicui, si homo sit a quo possit institui et deduci, et non curat alterius ductum amplecti.—*

§ *Nulli a Domino viam perfectionis ostendi, qui habens unde valeat erudiri, doctrinam seniorum et instituta contempserit, parvi pendens illud eloquium: interroga patrem tuum et annuntiabit tibi.—*Cassian.

source of ruin for souls, and that when you learn that a soul has fallen, it is no rash judgment to conclude that he willed to guide himself and have no other director but his own mind."—St. Dorothy.*

"We shall inevitably be overcome," says St. Ambrose, " if we have not a friend who consoles us in our afflictions, who re-animates us when discouraged, who rouses us from our languor, who, in a word, does for our soul what was formerly done for the paralytic by charitable persons who brought him to the feet of Jesus."

"The first thing which God requires of any one who aspires to sanctity is, that he renounce his own opinion, that is, that he humble himself and submit to the guidance of those to whom God has confided the ministry of souls. Just as there are very special graces attached to submission, so there are manifest dangers incurred when we have the pride to judge and govern ourselves. The interior life is full of obscurities, temptations, and pitfalls, and to enter it alone is evidently exposing one's self to the danger of being lost. Therefore there is no middle course :

---

*Ne persuademur esse nos satis ad regimen nostrum : opus est nobis auxilio præter Deum, opus est coadjutoribus.. nec aliter possit salvari.—

either we must absolutely renounce entering this life, or if God calls us thereto, we must take a director, that is, a man to whom we fully disclose our soul, to whom we render an account of everything pertaining to our spiritual life, and to whom, as God's representative, we render the obedience we would to God."—Grou. "Many," says the Venerable de la Salle, "lose the spirit and grace of their vocation because they do not fully disclose their heart to their superiors. If they do not observe this essential rule, it is impossible to guarantee them from the evil consequences liable to follow from the temptations with which the devil attacks those living in a community. These temptations are usually the stronger the more souls advance in virtue. For when they fervently labor to acquire the perfection of their state, the devil, who knows that if they persevere they will do him great harm, as much by their example as by the graces their prayers obtain for others, continually hovers about, watching, as St. Peter tells us, an opportunity to make them fall." "The enemy of our perfection rejoices" says St. Dorothy, "when he finds souls who trust to their own guidance and do not abandon themselves to the direction of their superiors, for he knows that they will fall like Autumn leaves, being alone in their struggle against him, or rather in league with him."

We could easily prolong these quotations which we find in great numbers in all books which treat of direction.

We will complete what we have cited, by the following remarkable page from Mgr. Rey, Bishop of Annecy. "Experience teaches us that the religious who ceases to follow direction under any pretext whatever, becomes lax, tepid, proud, arrogant, weak, sinful. 'He falls ill,' says St. Jerome, ' he does not make his malady known to the physician, therefore he cannot be cured, but dies.'

"Experience proves that a community, in which the rule for direction is not observed, goes ill, it is divided, it loses charity and religious simplicity—it falls into disorder. It is a fatal presage of more or less imminent dissolution.

"If it happen in a community that direction is no longer practised, or practised ill, I would say that such a community has run its course, it is lost. It must be regenerated and its soul restored, for *direction* is the soul of a community."

Necessity of Direction.

Proofs furnished by reason.

The necessity of a director in order to attain perfection is drawn :

1st. *From the very nature of a pious and perfect life.*

This life is a *divine art* by the exercise of which we become more and more submissive to Jesus Christ, and acquire a greater resemblance to our Divine Model.

Like all other sciences, it is usually only acquired by a knowledge of the elements, that is, the virtues of which it is composed, and the exercise of the virtues which, to be acquired and practised demand a more or less extended apprenticeship, and a habit which is sometimes formed only by heroic efforts.

Now, who is there, who, when he can easily have a master, would wish to learn by himself a science which is absolutely necessary to him in order to attain the end he proposes, particularly when the errors he is liable to commit in acquiring it may often be irreparable, and might, as in the present science, led him to perdition ?

2d. *The obstacles to be encountered in a devout life make a director necessary.*

The obstacles spring particularly from the

Necessity of Direction. 29

opposition within us to the practices of a devout life.

Thus, a devout life is a life of submission, and in us there is a decided tendency toward independence.

A devout life is a life of humility, a hidden life, and in us there is a decided tendency to vanity and an exterior life.

A devout life is a life of self denial, and in us there is a decided tendency to sensuality and sensual enjoyments. Therefore, continual effort on our part is required to struggle against these evil tendencies.

Now, who is capable, without counsel, of knowing how to struggle, and of finding means for the struggle? Who, without support, is capable of not falling off in his practice and of not being overcome?

These obstacles are also created by the evil one, who does not wish that we should attain this devout life, and foments troubles, temptations. discouragement, weariness, and other impediments.

How again, without an enlightened and experienced master are we to recognize and baffle the snares of the evil one?

The world also raises obstacles and opposes us with its mockeries or its joys; our family, our friends oppose us with their affection, our temperament opposes us with its delicacy. Again, how are we to resist these seductions, these allurements, these apparently absolute needs without a counsellor, a helper, a guide?

3d. *The illusions so frequently met with in a devout life, prove the necessity of a director.*

These illusions are snares by which the devil under the appearance of good, endeavors to lead to evil those who give themselves to virtue.

Who does not know how frequent are these illusions and how many souls they have ruined?

All our actions, the holiest in themselves, as well as the most indifferent, may, through the malice of the evil one, be fruitful in illusions.

They are to be found in austerities which we believe ourselves obliged to practice, which injuring our health, unfit us for the performance of our duty;—in the solitude which we believe ourselves obliged to observe to avoid the scandals of the world, and which prevent our performing the acts of zeal which, our duty prescribes;—in the prayers and meditation which we believe it our duty to prolong or multiply, or perform in a certain way under pretext of greater perfection;—in the acts of virtue, which we practice, thus zeal may be too ardent, humility too apparent, gentleness too inactive, etc.

There may also be illusions in what we call interior inspirations;—"without doubt these inspirations are precious," says St. Francis de Sales, "they are heavenly rays which bring into our hearts vivifying light which enables us to see the good and incites us to the pursuits of virtue and without them our souls would lead indolent, impotent, useless lives.

But who will assure us that these inspirations come from God, even when they incite us to an action which appears good to us, if it be but commanded by our rule, or is the result of our ordinary manner of life?

Frequently the devil in urging us to a good action and representing it as excessively important for our perfection, though it is not directly within the sphere of our duty, has no other object than to make us neglect a duty, yield to a thought of self complacency or inspire us with a feeling of compassion, perhaps contempt, for others apparently less divinely favored than ourselves.

"In order not to be deceived," says St. Fr. de Sales, " before heeding inspirations concerning important or extraordinary things, ask counsel of your guide that he may examine whether the inspiration be true or false. The enemy," adds the Saint, "seeing a soul prompt to accept inspirations, often suggests false ones to deceive her, which he never can do while she humbly obeys her confessor."

Illusions are never discerned by souls about whom they entwine their attractions, they can only be discovered by a clear sighted and disinterested friend, and even when discovered, their too weak, slothful, inconstant victims cannot dissipate them without the support, encouragement and firmness of a director.

4th. *The frequent and unexpected accidents encountered in the devout life make a director necessary.*

These accidents, or rather these maladies, which every pious soul experiences in a greater or less degree, and for a longer or shorter period are:

1st. *Discouragement* after a humiliating fall,—a failure which we deemed impossible,—a reproof, or sharp word which we think unmerited, or the apparent fruitlessness of our numerous efforts—How are we to keep up our courage and rise again, without a word from a friend who doubtless shows us the weakness of our virtue and that there is cause for humiliation, but also points out real amelioration in our conduct and persuades us to continue our efforts?

2d. *Aridity of mind and heart* when in neither one nor the other can be found a thought, a word, a sentiment, which leads it to God. Prayer wearies them, meditation particularly oppresses and tries them, communion seems useless, the exercise of virtues becomes very painful. . . How are we to continue the faithful performance of our duty without a friendly voice to tell us again and again that God is not obliged to console us, but that we are obliged to serve Him;—who will prove to us that joy, consolation, sensible fervor, do not give to prayer or action its real merit, but that it depends upon the will with which we act, and our efforts to act well.

3d. *Scruples.* There are sometimes long periods during which by a direct permission of God, or through the malice of the devil who often makes use of the weakness of our constitution, or in punishment for our infidelities and our little care to please God, our mental vision is obscured, we see nothing clearly or positively; everything we do seems a sin ;— a vague disquiet seizes our heart, our thoughts are unstable, our actions nerveless; we force ourselves to begin them, we leave them through fear of doing them ill, we resume them through fear of being punished by God. . . We suffer ourselves, and we make others suffer. How are we to come forth from this night which envelops us, without a hand which will hold us firmly and guide us with energy? Never was a scrupulous soul cured other than by submission to a director. *

4th. *Tepidity*, finally, which is more frequent and more dangerous than scruples and discouragement. We say our prayers badly through our own fault, we omit them without remorse, we merely try to pass away the time during meditation, and our little progress in virtue is a matter of indifference to us,— we do not positively wish to offend God, but we seek our own gratification on every occasion,— we do everything in our power to avoid suffering, and the end of all our efforts is to lead an easy life.—How are we to throw off this torpor without the energy of a director who, not only shows us the

---

* See at the end of the present work the Doctrine of St. Liguori on the necessity of a Director for *scrupulous souls*.

danger of our conduct, but impels and holds us to our duty and obliges us to perform it?

*

St. Bonaventure thus sums up the reasons which oblige a soul to have a director :

1. "A director is necessary to teach a soul what it should know—what it should fly, —what it should practice. Books no doubt tell us all these things, but some one must teach us to apply them to ourselves, otherwise our inclinations, our temperament, our very passions will modify the teachings of books in favor of our sensuality.

2. "A director is necessary to guide a soul in the practice of virtue. Knowledge is little, —will is a little more,—practice is everything; now, practice requires material aid to support, stimulate, to revive and encourage it. What soul is there which, left to itself, will not frequently exclaim: Enough, Enough! I can do no more!

3. " Every soul is a traveller who needs a guide.

"An invalid who needs a physician.

"A convalescent who needs some one to lean upon.

"An apprentice who needs a master."

II.

A Director is generally necessary for all kinds of persons, and for every one, whatever his condition,

Whether they are beginning, or whether they are advanced in perfection—whether they have already made great progress in virtue and find themselves in the ranks of the perfect. * *

*

Those who are beginning, need a director to purify themselves ; for as they themselves do not know all their maladies, and every one is constantly mistaken in things which concern himself, how can they cure themselves ?*

Even though they clearly recognized their infirmities and maladies, they could not efficaciously apply the remedies, for they would not take the special remedies, or they would take them indiscriminately, or finally they would weaken their effects by the almost inevitable mixture of self-will which corrupts all things.

"I beseech you, new plants of God," says St. Bernard, "you who do not ye

---

* Illud firmissime tenendum est difficillimum esse se ipsum cognoscere et curare, propterea quod naturaliter quisque seipsum amet.—S Basil.

discern good from evil, beware of following your own judgment; heed the counsels of those who have a greater knowledge than you of the artifices of the enemy, and who have acquired this knowledge by long and repeated experience, by all that they have felt themselves and witnessed in others."

"The Devil, that father of lies," says St. Justinian, " opposes his infernal views to the happy success of beginners, sometimes by sweet insinuations, sometimes by severe menaces; therefore, they need the guidance of a master who will not let them draw back with fear, or yield to seductions. Who, without experience, can avoid the snares of the unclean spirit? And who can have the experience without the counsels of a skilful master?" * *
*

Persons already purified, and advancing in virtue need a director to enlighten them : otherwise they incur great risk of wandering and being lost, for, "the way of salvation in the gospel is narrow, so narrow and so difficult" says St. Jerome, "that few find it, few enter it,—very few persevere therein."

The road of perfection resembles those little paths on the top of mountains bordered with precipices, where one can hardly take a step in safety, and without endangering his life—hence our mistakes in this road are frequent, perilous and difficult to repair.

We may be misled by *books* which, though good in themselves, may not suit us, or we may misunderstand them, therefore we need some one to choose and explain them for us.*

By *persons* whose society we frequent, therefore, we need some one to warn us.

By the *projects* we form of perfection, therefore, we need some one who will examine them.

By a too ardent or too slothful temperament, therefore we need some one who will calm, or rouse us....

These are the reasons which oblige us to take a guide in the spiritual life, and which prove the necessity of direction for those who desire to advance.

---

* It is particularly in the choice of books that we need a director....A good book is defined: " one which benefits the mind and heart without any risk to the religion or morality of the reader."

Now a book may be good in itself, yet dangerous to certain persons. At such an age with such a temperament, such a character, a book will do you no harm: but place the same book in the hands of a young person, trust it to a nature a'l fire, and the same work will have most disastrous effects.

" Ascetic books" says Father Faber, " are a terrible power: they can do as much harm as good, and, like steam, when they do harm the results are terrible....It is impossible to weave about one's self a stronger net of gross illusions than does he who reads spiritual books above his spiritual condition, or

Persons who aspire to perfection and who are already advanced, need the aid of a director to persevere, and become more perfect.

Perfection is nothing else but the perfect accomplishment of God's will, that is, without any mingling of our own will, just as the saints accomplish it in heaven.

Now, this is possible only in as far as our will is subject to a director who, holding the place of God, commands us in His name; for then only can we say with Christ, "I do not my will, but the will of my Father."

We need light and counsel in this state more than in any other.

The more advanced we are, the more the evil one multiplies temptations and snares.

"Those who are over others" says St. Bonaventure, "should submit to the direction

---

foreign to his actual wants. To every one who constantly reads books on mystical theology, the most ordinary state of prayer will appear extraordinary; a convert, particularly, will take common graces for rare favors. Of all realities, mystical theology is one of those in which it is easiest to take tinsel for gold. From constantly reading of a pure and disinterested love of God, we persuade ourselves that we have a like love in our hearts. Heroic thoughts are contagious, and we are soon inflated with them, but, they do not constitute practical heroism, they give at most a varnish of sentiment to our religion when there is no question of deeds and actions.

When a spiritual book does not contribute either to make us mortified or to keep us humble, it is sure to fill us with pride and turn us from the truth ; its doctrine goes to our head and we commit follies."

of another, in order to act with greater prudence and judgment; I except not even the Sovereign Pontiff." Eugenius III. submitted to the advice of St. Bernard. Our Lord, listening in the temple to the lessons given by the Doctors of the law, gives us an example of the humility, submission and simplicity with which we should seek and listen to counsel.

No one person has all the knowledge which it behooves man to possess, and God, to keep us in humility and paternal charity, is pleased to enlighten superiors in science and virtue by means of their inferiors.

" Suppose a religious possessed of all the light you will, he is nevertheless in need of a director. Illusions are so easy; a saint, a learned man, a wise religious, may be surprised by the snares of the devil, the errors of the world, a false and seductive ideal; for this reason, direction is necessary to all. St. Teresa was a genius, learned in the ways of God, much more so than her directors,

---

"Distrust," adds Mgr Landriot " all those lives filled with extraordinary things. Respect what the Church respects."

" We may even admire " says St. Fr. de Sales, " what we should never seek to imitate, but do not think that the Church approves all that circulates in the way of piety. "

With the exception of a few well known books : the *Imitation*, the *Spiritual Combat*, etc., let us ask advice concerning all those we have any desire to read.

but she nevertheless submitted to their direction."—Mgr. Rey.

III.
A Director is generally necessary in all spiritual states.

In times of fervor, to sustain us, that we may not attribute our progress to ourselves, that we may not despise, at least in our hearts, those who appear to be less faithful than ourselves, that we may not take as real fervor what is only a passing emotion of the heart, or the result of an exalted imagination.

In times of dryness, to sustain us, to encourage us, to help us to continue our duty in spite of weariness, weakness, discouragement; to practically teach us how to profit by this state of the soul and the merits we may acquire.

In times of joy, to keep us in moderation; in times of sadness, to uphold us.

At all times, to keep us in the way of perfection, and to bring us back when we have turned therefrom.

IV.
A Director is generally necessary to guide us in our various kinds of actions.

We have, in reality, but three kinds of actions to perform: those that are commanded, those that are counselled, and lastly, indifferent actions.

For those that are commanded, the Director encourages us, incites us to overcome the difficulties we meet in the performance of them,—regulates the time, the manner and other circumstances necessary to perform them well; and by this double obedience, our actions become more meritorious.

For the actions which are counselled, the Director indicates when they should be performed or omitted, according to the time, the person, and circumstances, and thus always maintains the soul in peace.

In the performance of indifferent actions, which are sometimes good, sometimes bad, sometimes useful, sometimes injurious and dangerous, who can be sure that he is not influenced by fancy, caprice, vanity or sensuality, if he have not a director who reassures him by tracing a rule of conduct to follow? Then happy the souls who can say at every hour, every moment: I am not guided by my caprice or humor, but by obedience. —Whether I succeed or fail, whether my actions be approved or blamed by men, what mattereth it! God will count it in heaven for me, for I do it in obedience to His will.

Let us conclude this Chapter with the following words from Tronson :

"The necessity of a director,—the account we should render him,—the manner in which we should depend upon his guidance, is a matter which flesh and blood cannot digest, human prudence can with difficulty understand it, the wise of this world cannot submit to it, and yet the holy fathers believed it of such importance that they presented it to Christians as you present the alphabet to children, to teach them to read, that is, as one of the first elements of Christianity, and one of the first principles necessary to learning the Gospel.

CHAPTER SECOND.

Advantages of Direction.

1st. Advantages to a community.

1. The life, the well being, the sanctity of a community depend upon the union of its members and the harmony with which they all labor for the same end. This unity and harmony are only possible in proportion as each member with his individual temperament—individual faults, individual views, endeavors to modify what is his own that he may attain to the one mind common to all the members of the community.

It is a difficult and important labor which can only be successfully achieved under the influence of direction and of one director.

I.

2. The director who, by the avowal we make to him, not of our sins, as we shall show later, but of our tendencies, our faults, our efforts, and who gradually learns the tem-

perament of each one whom he directs, takes from one, adds to another, moderates a third, rouses a fourth, and thus produces a certain concurrence of thought and action which in spite of inevitable deviations, makes the community one in its purpose.

Just as the rule to which all submit modifies bodily habits and produces exterior regularity, so this single *impetus* given to all produces a certain resemblance.

3. The director knowing the aptitude and tastes of each member of the community can, when he is superior, so distribute the functions and charges, so unite different members in their labors, as to develop for the common good, all the gifts of strength and knowledge which God has given to each one.

If the superior does not know his subjects, or knows them imperfectly, he will give charges to those who appear capable of filling them, or believe themselves capable though lacking the necessary qualifications; he will leave two religious together who cannot labor in unison, or whose sympathy is such that it may interfere with their progress in virtue, he will make appointments which will perhaps injure the whole community.

Religious administration requires a far-seeing and correct judgment, which is attainable only through good direction ; and, if this direction is practised as it should be, then appointments, removal, changes, everything, will turn to the advantage of the community in general, and of each member in particular.

"After examining the subject before God," writes St. Ignatius in his *Constitutions*, " it seemed to us in presence of the Divine Majesty, that it was extremely fitting that all the religious should make themselves perfectly known to their superior, in order that the latter may more easily direct those who are under their guidance,—preserve them from all danger,—and more easily provide for the good of all."

" Direction is a double power," says Mgr. Rey," a power of formation, a power of attraction."

By wise direction, souls are formed to good, to virtue, to the religious state, and perfected therein.

By wise direction, souls are attracted to God by an interior spirit, a spirit of prayer, a spirit of faith.

Now, for a religious, formation and attraction constitute everything.

II.

Unless the direction in the community be uniform, it will only result in agitation. There will be many individual efforts, few general results, many virtues and even individual sanctity, but little general edification.

Unless direction be uniform there will be a universal discomfort, but little accord, in spite of good will on the part of the members, no love for one another, notwithstanding exterior marks of politeness and even acts of charity.

Unless direction be uniform, the community will be divided by parties, particular friendships will abound, and perhaps, even cabals.

In direction, complaints, murmurs, misunderstandings, resentments, little prejudices are buried never to re-appear again.

We seek direction with our heart embittered, we unburden our soul with perfect freedom, and we return to our labors, if not cured, at least calmed and strengthened.

A year of direction faithfully accepted by a whole community would completely transform it.

And if novitiates are more fervent, it is because they observe the rule concerning direction with greater simplicity and regularity.

1st. Advantage to the individual.

I.

Direction opens the heart.

Direction is also called opening the heart, and in this respect it is particularly advantageous.

There are times in life when the heart has need to unburden itself.

It is oppressed with a burden, sometimes of memories,—regrets,—weariness,—temptations,—sadness,—a need to love which tortures it with a dull pain and makes life weary and hard to endure.

For these trials there is but one remedy: an outpouring of the heart. *

Founders of Orders who knew these trials and their sole remedy, have, therefore, instituted direction.

If direction is not accessible, the sick heart will seek among those about it or perhaps abroad a sympathetic friend; and thence results a wholly natural friendship which gradually dissipates its spirit of piety

---

* " He who keeps his sorrow to himself," says St. Thomas, " feels it more keenly, for he is much more occupied with it ; when he makes it known, his attention is distracted from it, and he is much relieved, for the attention thus shared with another enlarges his heart and causes it to find some solace."

Advantages of Direction. 49

and ends by becoming culpable ; or if this heart dare not unburden itself to anyone, it will abandon itself to sadness, to weariness, to laxness, to sensuality.

II.

Direction dilates the heart.

It enlarges it and renders it capable, so to speak, of comprehending and embracing God.

Who has not felt at times that his heart was sealed against everything? We cannot explain this iron band, which seems to encompass our poor heart, but we feel that it closes it to every good thought, every pure affection, every joy. Direction breaks this iron fetter and our heart expands and breathes with freedom.

It was not only a confessor that it needed, but a friend... the friend of a religious is called a director. No one can console himself; consolation is essentially social.

Ah! who may express the joy, the happiness of a dilated heart! Creatures pass but do not dwell therein; trials and anxieties doubtless make themselves felt but they abide not, and leave only their merits.

A dilated heart is a field where God, undeterred by any rival, sows His harvest of virtues.

III.

Direction gives peace.

He who puts himself under direction, places his soul, in a measure, in the hands of another who has the divine mission to lead him to heaven.

Then, no more fears, no more anxiety... The soul has not to ask: Am I in the right way? Have I sufficient contrition for my sins? Am I not laboring under a delusion? No, it no longer needs to ask these questions. It has opened its heart simply and frankly, and obeys with the same simplicity and frankness:—it is told to walk, it walks; it is told to halt, it halts Why should it be disquieted? "Direction" said a good, devout soul, "is a carriage into which we need only enter to go straight to heaven."

But there are some who fear direction: it is not solid, it is not sure;—there are some who disdain it: it is not to my taste, I would like other means...

Then go on foot, you who will not trust yourselves to God...

"One cannot do wrong in obeying," says Rodriguez. "The spiritual superior may, in commanding you to do certain things; but you are sure of not erring in obeying his command, for God will only ask you whether you have done what you were commanded, and provided you can render a good account thereof, you will be wholly acquitted."

"Servants of God, both men and women," exclaims a pious author, "understand at last the marvellous security God has so abundantly bestowed upon you in your obedience to a confessor. O ineffable words! This mortal, your fellow creature, is not infallible it is true, but you yourselves are infallible each time you obey him, and God has solemnly pledged Himself never to reproach you with anything you may have done or omitted under obedience.

"Present yourself to him with a determined will to accept what he prescribes, to reject what he forbids, and I will answer to God for everything

"Do you not understand that this disposition on your part essentially excludes the will to sin, without which, no act whatever can be a sin. And after this, what remains in our conduct for the good and just God whom we serve, to condemn and punish?

"The decision of a confessor establishes us in perfect good faith, and were you, in obedience to him, to do a thing which seemed to you forbidden, your good faith would change such an action into a praiseworthy deed, and render it worthy of heavenly reward just as much as alms-giving or the most laudable penances."

If it be true, as we read in *Les Avis Spirituels*, that virtue consists in perfect submission to the will of God,—in renouncing ourselves,—in distrusting and being detached from our own lights, God who is so good, cannot but be touched when a soul will say to Him: "Thou knowest that I cannot guide myself. I have chosen as guides those whom I believed capable of teaching me to love Thee; I obey them because it is Thou whom I behold in their person; I come to Thee at their word which I regard as an order from Thee; wilt Thou punish me, my God, for having tried to obey Thy will? If Thou hadst willed me to guide myself, Thou wouldst have increased my light; but Thou hast made me blind; Thou art too just to condemn me for having sought a guide and believed him as I would Thee."

What peace, what tranquillity these reflections must leave in the soul! What a feeling of security, when the Director, on the part of God, says : "Go in peace!—Be at rest! I charge myself with your salvation before God!"

IV.

Direction causes us to advance in virtue.

Human sciences cannot be acquired without a master,—nor can the science of salvation be acquired without a master.

Never was a man formed to anything whatever by himself.

God is doubtless supreme Master, but He wills, as we have said, to make use of the ministry of man in the sanctification of man, and He tells us as he did Saul: "Go to Ananias, he will tell thee what thou must do."

Direction raises us when we have fallen, encourages us, stimulates us, and gives good example ;—its work is more minute than that of confession ; it studies the exterior conduct and brings to our attention faults which we overlook. It acts in concert with the soul in its efforts to overcome its evil inclinations. Direction requires not so much humiliating avowals, which are reserved for confession, as a knowledge of our efforts to overcome certain inclinations, to surmount certain weaknesses, to resist certain temptations ; and these efforts, however slight, are recalled by direction from time to time in order to sustain us, and excite us to continue. Moreover, when we know that we must give our director an account of our prayer and our communion, of what method we have followed, and what fruit we have drawn therefrom ;—of the penances we perform, and the mortifications we practice, of our labor, of our readings, of our relations with others—of all our actions, intentions, projects, it is impossible that this thought should not incite us to be more faithful and to devote ourselves more earnestly to the pursuit of virtue.

All that not only Saints, but also philosophers, seeking only to perfect human nature, have said of the advantages of particular examen, that is, of that daily introspection of the soul seeking its failings to repair them,—its weaknesses to avoid them,—good actions to perfect them,—may be said with more truth of direction, which is a particular examen made by two. The director brings to the assistance of the soul in pursuit of its faults, his experience, his light, and above all, his impartiality, which is too often wanting in particular examen.

He brings also the support of his counsels, the sweetness of his friendship, the strength of his encouragement.

Oh! in truth, even in a human point of view, who would not have a friend to care for his soul as his mother cared for his temporal needs?

A director is such a friend; thus does St. Francis de Sales name him, paraphrasing for him the sweet words of the Bible: "He will be to us" he says, "a treasure of wisdom in our afflictions, in our falls, in our discouragement,—he will serve us healing remedies to lleviate and console our hearts in their spiritual maladies, he will preserve us from evil and perfect the good in us,—and when we are overtaken with any infirmity, he will prevent its being mortal, for he will restore us."

It will be useful to develop these thoughts.

V.

Direction causes us to taste on earth the joys of holy friendship.

Direction is the practice of friendship in its sweetest, strongest, purest, most consoling, most useful sense.

Only this friendship does not unite two hearts so much as two souls.

And if for this reason it is devoid of that natural sensibility which thrills one at the mere sight of a friend, it also loses that which forms the danger of human friendship : an attachment which frequently becomes passionate,—a somewhat sensual enjoyment, innocent, no doubt, but which nevertheless has the effect of weakening the impressions of grace,—a too ardent affection which converts two friends into two beings living apart in themselves and by this very fact wounding fraternal charity.

Affection forms the basis of direction and of friendship, it is the atmosphere in which they both live. But the end of friendship is to love and be loved ; it gives and in return wishes to receive ; the end of direction is to perfect and to sanctify. Loving and being loved form only a means.

The Christian Mother unites in herself the two elements which form the essence of direction and friendship.

Friendship equalizes hearts ; persons who love, would see and feel and speak alike . . . and involuntarily this equality is established. In direction there is always a difference between the soul directing and the soul directed. The director bends, inclines, he does not descend, he bends to take the soul and raise it, sometimes to a degree of perfection which he has not attained himself, for he receives for others, graces which he may not have received for himself.

Friendship springs spontaneously; it is more the effect of instinct than of reason; at least it begins through instinct, and reason only follows afterwards. It has need to supernaturalize its intentions and its motives, not to fall into forgetfulness of God and its duties.—Direction, particularly in religious communities, is accepted, reasons, questions, and cannot live and bear fruit but by the spirit of faith.

The ties of both have a different source: sympathy is the bond of friendship, faith is the bond of direction, but they both become equally sweet and powerful. The spirit of faith is more lasting and less susceptible than sympathy.

Friendship naturally seeks more or less mutual pleasure and enjoyment. It must have become very holy before it can determine to pain a friend with a correction; it is difficult for it to understand that it must sometimes wound in order to heal. Direction seeks only the sanctification of a soul, and in administering a reproof, carefully no doubt, and with all the sweetness of charity, loses sight of the pain it causes, in the result it would obtain, viz.: the perfection of the soul confided to its care.

Friendship is one of the charms of life ; when it unites two hearts they seem raised above all sorrows. Direction has not this charm which, in a human sense, may be translated emotion. It is even painful at times, for it is a duty, and God has attached some pain to duty to make it richer in merit, but how sweet are the joys it brings to the soul!

The soul is at peace concerning the past ; she has sincerely laid bare her spiritual condition ; her wounds have been healed ; think no more of the past, she is told, and she tranquilly obeys.

The soul is at peace concerning the future; she knows that this guidance is leading her to heaven, and, notwithstanding the anxieties which may sometimes trouble her, she can say with confidence: God will not permit obedience to direction to lead me astray.

The soul is at peace concerning the present, she feels that she has the support of a strong, pure friendship, even though no word of affection be uttered, and that her weaknesses, her faults, or even her waywardness can never weaken this friendship while she continues to be simple, docile, humble and confiding.

How could she not be happy ?

* *
*

Finally to conclude :

1st. Direction causes us to see our faults, and helps us to correct them.

2d. It is a sovereign remedy against all temptations. " The humility which leads us to make known our temptations is so pleasing to God," says Cassian, "that not only does He cause us to find in it a remedy for our troubles, but frequently, even before the Director has spoken, the evil one loosens his hold and the temptation vanishes.

3d. It enables us to practice virtue with greater facility, and preserves us from the illusions of our own mind. " What must one do to advance in virtue ?" said a young religious to St. Antony:—" Let yourself be guided, and obey ;" replied the Saint.

4th. It renders us constant in our good resolutions, for the obligation alone, of rendering an account of all our actions, is a powerful incentive to do well.

5th. It is a great source of consolation in the trials and critical situations in which we sometimes find ourselves, because of the support, encouragement and counsel we receive.

After reading these two Chapters, may we not conclude that there ought to be very few souls who should refuse to submit to direction?

No, there are none among you, dear souls, who, though weak, even culpable, and filled with a thousand faults perhaps, yet have a good will, and desire at any price to please God and become Saints.

The few who rebel against direction, who ridicule it, and seek to turn others from it, are proud souls, convinced of their own sufficiency— slothful, sensual souls, taking little pains to advance— touchy, suspicious souls, fearing to be too well known, to be reproved, to be too little appreciated, and who silence their conscience with : Direction after all is not commanded under pain of sin.

We will return later to these poor souls who voluntarily resist God's voice calling them to perfection.

CHAPTER THIRD.

Choice of a Director.

The director may be the confessor or another priest, or finally, in communities, the superior, who may not, or who cannot be a priest, as in communities of women.

In communities, the director is usually appointed ; outside of communities, one is free to choose a director.

I.

An appointed Director.

This Chapter specially concerns communities. Here the choice of a director is made by the rule which prescribes that every religious shall at certain fixed times go to his or her director to give him what St. Francis de Sales calls " the account of the month," and what in other communities is called, account of " conscience." We know all the complaints and objections to which this obligation of manifesting one's soul to a person appointed gives rise. We will answer some of these objections later.* When there is question of confession, our spirit of faith, which is livelier and stronger in the reception of the sacraments, enables us to overcome any natural repugnance; then too the confessor is not seen, and does not see, but when there is question of that manifestation of conscience which, in some communities is a *tête à tête*, there are temperaments which cannot bring themselves to speak or reply. Direction, to some souls, is real torture; in these cases, it might perhaps, be well for superiors to dispense such souls temporarily from this point of the rule. Freedom of heart is the essence of direction; "direction," says Father Faber, "should be free as air."

The time given to this exercise may be spent in giving counsel, encouragement, or even in pious reading.

Prayer on the part of the director and the soul directed will end by bringing about that confidence which cannot be forced, but is a grace of God. Happy are confiding souls, particularly in religion!

To souls whose temperament makes it repugnant for them to seek direction in the

---
* See Chapter vi.

Choice of a Director.

usual way, I shall simply say : Try to overcome yourselves through a spirit of faith, prepare in writing, if necessary, what you have to say, and remember that this direction, which costs you so much to seek, is the safest and most meritorious.

* *
*

The following reflections apply equally to the ordinary confessor, who is also appointed, and about whom the evil one accumulates difficulties which appear insurmountable.

Here also we understand how painful is this forced confidence, so to speak ; it is perhaps one of the heaviest crosses of the religious life, when God permits it to be imposed. But, poor soul, bending under its weights, what a continual occasion of merit it will be for you, if you accept with resignation! How it will cause God to forget your frequent resistance to grace, your infidelity to good inspirations, your frequent seeking of self, even in your pious exercises, and former, perhaps too human attachments, which you sought with so much eagerness!

No doubt, the very fact, sometimes, that a confessor or director is appointed, prevents our finding in him, whatever his merits, that sympathy which cheers the soul; it creates even a certain restraint, which paralyzes the frank confidence we would give him, and a certain repugnance which, if allowed to grow, gradually becomes unconquerable... But this confessor and this director are sent us by God to sanctify us, and God tells us: "I desire that thou shouldst go to him, he has for thy soul all the graces which at this present moment are necessary for it, go to him, then, and heed him."

Do you think that if you seek direction, or go to confession under obedience, doing all that depends upon you to fulfil your duty, God will not reward you for this almost heroic act?

Wait patiently, labor in difficulties and tears, carefully hiding from others all that you suffer, and when the proper time shall have come, God will send you, either during the Ember days, or a retreat, or in a wholly providential manner, one of His angels who has a special mission to restore, strengthen and comfort souls, and who in an hour, thanks to the preparation your soul has undergone through resignation, will make you advance more than you would in a whole year of confession and direction in accordance with your desires.

How often must pious persons be told that he who has charge of their soul, director or confessor, is only the channel of God's light and grace. And he whom God sends, has for them the graces of sanctification and perfection which they now require.

Then, understand what God asks of you. It is neither the sanctity of your director, nor the confidence he inspires, but your docility, which will save you. You will perhaps allege that, if St. Teresa had not had another director she would probably have been lost. But remember, 1st, that God gave her another, as he will you, when the proper time comes, were it necessary to bring one from a distant country; 2d, God rewarded her for her submission; 3d, God, finally, would never require virtues of her which, through a want of knowledge, she might have been unable to practice.

Hear, moreover, St. Teresa's avowal in her own words: " The guidance of my director was very injurious to me.... but that was no excuse for me before God....and I think God permitted, in punishment of my sins, that my directors should be deceived themselves and deceive me...." See what she adds after this avowal: " When His Divine Majesty commanded me something in prayer, and my confessor told me the contrary, God recommended me to obey my confessor." Let these words be your great rule. "God," continues St. Teresa, "brought it about that my confessor afterward commanded me what His Divine Majesty had told me to do. God wished me to conceal nothing from my confessor. Here is a great safeguard."

Sometimes, because of our imagination, our prejudices, our inconstancy, our love of novelty, and the need we have of sensible impressions to believe we are advancing, we seem to profit more by the extraordinary director of inferior merit, than by the ordinary confessor, who no longer produces any sensible effect in us. That may be; but do you know the reason? It is because your ordinary confessor has prepared your soul in spite of you, and without your knowledge.... God rarely works sudden miracles. He wishes that the soil be prepared for Him.

We must give here, in relation to the direction of Superiors in communities of women, a few pages, full of practical teaching, from *Lettres sur la Vie Réligieuse :*

"You will remit the care of your conscience to the priest; you will go to him at certain fixed periods, that is, every fortnight, to lay your faults at his feet and to receive his counsels and the precious succors of his ministry; but is it to him also that you should address yourself for what we more specially call *direction?* No, my dear daughter; religion, which knows your wants, your weakness, your constant need of succor, has placed near you a permanent guide, who is ever within your reach; this guide is your superior, she is the source you must seek, the torch which must burn to light your path; and how many claims she has to your confidence! She is born in your midst, so to speak, rocked in the same cradle, nourished with the same food, she has followed the path you are following, encountered the same obstacles. The rule is her daily study, her ordinary reading; her administration has ripened her experience, she has every means of being enlightened before she gives a counsel, she is surrounded with the confidence of her sisters by whose suffrages she has been placed at their head; therefore she has every right to receive your confidence, to know your needs, and every means of satisfying them.

" Her ministry,—shall I venture to say it?—her ministry may be even more useful to you than that of a priest. He only sees you in passing, during a few short moments; he seizes with difficulty and hastily, a few traits of your character, a few of your tendencies; she sees you constantly, she is with you every day, she studies you, she examines you, the precipitation of a first judgment, is corrected by the maturity of a second; she can more surely confirm her ideas, and consequently be more useful to you.

"The priest only knows what you tell him, he must believe your deposition; he applies remedies accordingly, and may err through no fault of his, but because he does not know you well. You, yourself, may be deceived and represent yourself inaccurately. A superior will have a knowledge, not only of what you tell her, but even of what you have forgotten or omitted to tell her; you will hardly need to speak, your malady is already known to her; she has seen its origin, followed its progress, calculated its chances; she will not be anxious, if there is no cause for anxiety; she will reassure you, console you, dissipate your anxiety, revive your drooping courage, or extend a helping hand to you when you are on the point of falling.

"The priest only sees you at remote periods; the rule forbidding you to seek him more frequently without permission, he can only see you in the holy tribunal, the time he does give you must be short, to avoid the appearance of preference, and not to keep waiting an eager multitude pressed by numerous occupations, who might murmur and complain. Therefore he can only counsel you hastily, without giving you time to develope your difficulties. A superior is with you every day, she can give you all the time you need, she is constantly at hand, you can consult her the moment any difficulty occurs.

Moreover, not unfrequently, by the time you reach the holy tribunal, the trouble has passed, calm is restored, and you are astonished at the anxiety with which you were filled. Understand then, my daughter, all the assistance you may derive from the direction of your superior.

" The ministry of the priest is doubtless higher, sacramental graces are attached thereto ; but the superior also is clothed with a ministry, she also has gifts which are proper to her : if her ministry is less sublime, it is at least maternal. If she is mature in age, she will offer you the experience of her years; if she is still young, she will be more energetic, more bold, and perhaps, more urgent in her zeal; if she even is subject to little miseries and little weaknesses, let not your confidence be shaken; the divine Master willed to place at the head of His Church two apostles, one of whom denied Him and the other persecuted the infant Church, in order, perhaps, that they might be more compassionate. It is also for that reason age and sorrow are always more indulgent, for they have acquired compassion or experience.

"Finally, a true reflection ; if God on the one hand promises to reward our faith, and our simplicity, on the other, He grants light and grace to her whom He sends to us. Frequently luminous thoughts present themselves to her mind, words escape her which impress hearts so deeply that she cannot but recognize the effect of the assistance promised by the divine Master to those who are to speak in His name. Therefore, you will address yourself particularly to the mother superior, since she has the mission and the grace to guide you."

There may, nevertheless, be certain cases, and the rule has provided for them, when other direction may be more profitable ; the prudence of the superior meets such cases, and you have only to continue simple and obedient. But there is no case in which a sister may of herself, unless by express permission, choose one of her companions to direct her. Her talents, her piety inspire you with confidence ; that may be, but she will always lack indispensable qualifications : —she has neither the mission nor the authority for her work, and thus experience proves that such direction always degenerates into particular friendships which are the pests of religious communities.

II.

Freedom in the choice of a Director.

When we are free to choose a director we must understand that this choice is not usually the result of an impression, an attraction, nor to be hastily made.

It is certain, first of all, that the greater number of souls need no other director than a confessor, and that in the world there are few souls who need take any trouble to obtain special direction. Confession, according as it is made, the questions of the priest, and the counsels he gives, may suffice. Guilloré even says that "usually the director and confessor should be the same, for there are many things which should only be communicated under the veil of the sacrament, and which, nevertheless, are necessary for direction. This separate direction frequently causes great abuses, for while the confessor has only a knowledge of ordinary things relating to the soul, a knowledge of the heart and a hundred little confidences are given the director. I acknowledge, however, that there may be certain circumstances in which for good reason, which I leave to the judicious discernment of those concerned, one may have a director independently of his confessor."

Even in communities the ordinary and extraordinary confessor would be sufficient to direct souls, were it not necessary for the superior to know his subjects, to replace the priest, when absent, not to remit sin, doubtless, but to enlighten a scrupulous conscience, dissipate a cloud which troubles one before communion, or to form the religious to the particular spirit of the community, with which the confessor sometimes is not sufficiently familiar; or possibly, even to incite his subjects to greater progress with more authority and wisdom,— or finally, in order to give each one the employment suited to his ability and acquirements.

For the reasons just stated, founders of Orders have established monthly direction outside of confession.

Choice of a Director.

More care and attention are required in the choice of a director than of a confessor.

When we have only to declare our sins and receive absolution, if we are sincerely sorry for our faults and firmly determined to avoid the occasion of them, and to take precautions not to fall again, we have no need to be troubled, particularly when it is only occasionally that we need the ministry of a priest.

The direct end of confession being to cure the wounds made by sin, the power conferred by Holy Orders, and the jurisdiction granted by the Bishop, suffice for the Sacrament, provided the conditions necessary on our part are not wanting.

The end of direction being, as we said, to perfect the soul by gradually destroying the faults which rule it,—to beautify it by teaching it to acquire virtues,—to enable it to fully correspond to God's designs,— the director must be possessed of piety, knowledge, experience. This is the teaching of the Roman Catechism. The faithful, it tells us, ought to understand how careful they should be to choose as confessors, priests commendable by the integrity of their lives, knowledge, and prudence of judgment.

1. With piety, which keeps the director near

the Divine Master, he will attract you to God.

He will have only the interests of your soul in view, your temporal affairs will only concern him incidentally; he will seek neither your approbation, nor your affection, but lead you direct to God : he will labor for you with zeal, for he will understand the importance of enabling a soul to attain the degree of perfection to which God calls it,— with charity, which he will know is pleasing to God, a charity perfectly free from weakness, cowardice, or any material consideration.

2. Knowledge will show him your present state,—the paths you should follow,—the special exercises you should practice, the illusions to which you are liable.

"Our director" says St. Teresa, "should be pious and learned; but if we cannot find these two qualities united, it is better to take one who is learned, rather than one who is pious but not learned."

"Of all the wise sayings of this illustrious Saint" adds Fr. Faber, "I know none in which her character is better reflected than in this."

"I have always believed," the great Saint adds, "and will always believe that every Christian should seek as director, a man versed in spiritual science : the more learned he is, the more beneficial will he be ; those who are called to certain states of prayer particularly need such a director. I firmly believe that a soul called to certain degrees of prayer, who consults a learned director, will not, unless she wishes to deceive herself, be misled by the illusions of the devil."

3. Experience of the things of God will give more firmness to the director's doctrine, and make his counsels more clear.

A learned confessor may guide a soul in all that concerns religion, and prevent it from going astray ; but a person of experience only can help you to walk in the way of perfection.

We have no need to dwell further on the qualities necessary to a director, nor particularly to mention with more detail the marks by which we may recognize whether a director be possessed of piety, learning, and the necessary experience.

Such details might be prejudicial to certain self-sufficient souls who judge, compare, criticise, and, imparting their impressions to others, injure the ministry of those who do not meet with their approval.

What mistaken judgments are created by

opinions founded on mere impressions! How many priests have seen their ministry paralyzed by the criticism of pious souls to whom their general appearance was not pleasing!

Let us not seek so much, but pray with simplicity, and wait!

God is pledged not to fail souls who seek Him with an upright intention.

* *
*

How will you know that such a person is the director you need? I cannot say, but I know that if you are faithful, if you pray, if you are firmly determined to submit, to be humble, to allow yourself to be guided, God will make him known to you among the thousands from whom St. Fr. de Sales tells us a director should be chosen. "Earnestly ask God to send you a director after His heart, and doubt not that He will send you a good and faithful one, rather, He will send you an angel as He did the young Tobias; but you must ask it long and earnestly, as the greatest favor God can bestow upon you, for a wise director is the channel through which God communicates all His graces to souls." The employment of up-

Choice of a Director.

right human measures is, doubtless not forbidden. "Seek information," says Fenelon, "from persons who are most simple, most solid, and least influenced by vain appearances, and whose conduct leads you to hope that you will profit by the counsels of him whom you wish to choose... It is even necessary, if possible, to see and converse several times with the director we wish to choose, that we may learn whether we can go to him with the necessary frankness and openness, and whether we will find in him all that we need to find... Then simply follow what God puts into your heart; good will, simplicity, detachment from all self interests, the fear of falling into hands which are not the best for God's designs, finally, confidence in grace, will be your guides.

"God will see your heart and will give you according to the measure of your faith. Let your only object in seeking a director be, to die to yourself without reserve, and to hold to nothing in this life. God, who never fails an upright heart, will gratify the desire of your soul; an angel Raphael will be sent you.

"Humble yourself, be detached from all your own interests, remove from your heart all that could prevent you from being docile, and the guide you seek will not be denied you. 'He will come, I know not how, but he will come.' A conversation, a chance, a trifle, will open your eyes, and you will see him for whom you are waiting."

* *
*

A soul under direction may, doubtless, find faults in her director; but if she have the proper spirit of piety, she will see them without remarking them; she will attribute them to human weakness, remembering, that no one is exempt from faults,—that a fault is not necessarily a vice,—that God leaves the most eminent directors with even apparent faults, that knowing their own miseries, they may have more compassion for those of others;—that a man may be very holy, with defects, against which he unceasingly struggles,—that the director, finally, being God's organ, we must not stop at him, but rise by means of him to God, and that our contempt for his person reflects upon God Himself, whom he represents.

St. Teresa was more learned in the ways of God than her directors, and yet with what simplicity she exposed her doubts! with what humility she listened !—with what obedience she submitted !

* *
*

We find in an excellent book published by a Dominican, * the following pages which may perhaps enlighten some souls troubled about the choice of a director: "For some time the soul of Herminie seemed to be hovering between several paths ; she went from one to the other, not knowing which to choose ; she hesitated and was troubled concerning her duty. An indefinite uneasiness like that which besets a traveller, uncertain of his route, impelled her to seek a guide more familiar with heavenly things, and more skilful in sounding the depths of our nature, that she might be enlightened by his counsels and find support in his strength.

"This change was very trying to her, not that she was influenced by these considerations, more common than we think, which paralyze so many souls : what will my confessor say ? Will I not give him pain ? Is not this ingratitude ? No, Herminie lived in too elevated an atmosphere for these

---

* *Herminie de la Bassemouturie*, par le P. Thomas des frères Prêcheurs.

purely human considerations to reach her. Her fears came from a better source, a profound respect for the Priest. With the penetration which faith and humility give, she understood all the sublimity of the priestly vocation.

"The miseries and infirmities inseparable from everything human, mingled with what is divine, escaped her, or at least only appeared to her lost in the mysterious splendor of his divine character. The slightest unfavorable criticism of a Priest, uttered in her presence, pained her.

"If a school friend ventured an unbecoming remark, she never hesitated to say : 'Ah! if our Mothers heard you!'

"Later, she thus retraces for herself the mission of the Priest : 'Oh! how I love, how I venerate the Priest, God's servant, the minister of the Divinity ; the Priest raised by sacerdotal grace above the angels ; the Priest who daily holds in his hands the Saviour of the world, Jesus Christ, whom he represents on earth ! The Priest, the friend of God, the friend of man, the mediator between God and man, and who unceasingly bears messages from one to the other : he is the dispenser of bread to the poor, of comfort to the sick, of consolation to the afflicted. He is ever, and at all times, the father and the providence of all.

"At our birth the Priest makes us children of heaven by giving us light and grace. At our death, it is again the Priest who helps us to pass the bounds of the last and terrible passage ; he encourages us at this dread moment, he exhorts us, and, reclothing us a last time in the robe of innocence, opens to us the gates of eternal life.

"And during the short space which separates the cradle from the tomb, how frequently have we to bless the hand of the Priest ever extended to his unfortunate brothers? How often has this venerated hand poured balm on our wounds, dissipated our fears, banished our sadness? How many times has this paternal hand withdrawn us from the abyss? Yes, when the ties which bind us to heaven are broken, the Priest weeps like a father over the sorrows of a son. Sustained by his great heart, he prays, and with touching patience and perseverance, labors to repair the misfortune. His gentle, firm words follow the traces of the evil and efface it, he restores what was fallen and fortifies it ; he warms what was cold, and reunites between father and son the ties which were so sadly severed.

"And to speak but of ourselves, it was through one of these worthy ministers that God restored peace and serenity to our days, and with these blessings the joy and health which we had ceased to know. After the death of a father, a mother, and beloved brothers, when prostrated by our sorrow, it was this hand which raised us up; at its touch we felt new life, a smile returned to our lips, and our tearful eyes were raised in fervent gratitude to heaven for the gift we had received."

Herminie's veneration for the Priest, based upon these various motives, a veneration which manifested itself by a modest and reserved bearing, and a childlike confidence, inspired her with such an invincible repugnance to any idea of change, that nothing short of her keen uneasiness could make her decide to examine the delicate question of choosing a new director. St. Francis de Sales consulted, tells her: "Choose him among a thousand." St. Teresa affords her some reasons drawn from her own experience: "Even though your confessor be intelligent and learned, endeavor to go to another from time to time... I know that there are many to whom this is profitable."

St. John and St. Paul manifest the use-

Choice of a Director. 83

fulness of a good director when they show us that our Lord gives to His Church, workmen of every stamp formed by that Spirit which breathes where He will, which gives without measure, but with discrimination; who makes some Apostles, and some Prophets, and other some Evangelists, and other some pastors and doctors, for the perfecting of the Saints, for the work of the ministry, for the edifying of the body of Christ, giving us to understand by these words that there must likewise be a hierarchy in directors of souls, some being more interior, more spiritual, more experienced, and therefore, more capable of safely guiding us to perfection, the sole end of all our efforts. These high authorities were needed to terminate Herminie's hesitation ; accustomed to decide in everything only after she had consulted God in prayer, she will be careful of permitting herself to yield to I know not what natural instinct which too often becomes the sole motive in the very important choice of the Father of our soul. She withdraws into herself, she invokes the Holy Spirit; how many times does she not say : " Give me I beseech Thee, O my God, a sure and enlightened guide who will lead me to Thy love, who will guide me in the path of perfection ; and if to attain this it be necessary to traverse forests of thorns, to ford deep torrents, to wander through nameless deserts, I accept in advance all the trials of the route, relying on Thy powerful succor which never fails one who trusts in Thee."

And again :

" I have always had a great desire to love Thee with all my heart, O my sweet Master! but this desire now seems less vague, it is united more firmly with my will and I feel that it must cease to be fruitless. I desire then, to take means of testifying this love as much and as perfectly as possible, but of myself I can do nothing ; and I must needs repeat: Lord, what wilt thou that I do? O how willingly I should obey him who would consent to guide my soul! But is this precious friend to be found ? Cause me to find him, O my God, and while waiting to speak to me by his lips, speak to my heart, enlighten my understanding, above all strengthen my will, for I feel my weakness and my misery to be extreme. "

She added to these prayers novena upon novena ; finally she rose, and impelled by a secret inspiration from God, found the guide whom she sought. He was an enlightened priest, whose prudent and firm direction caused her to advance rapidly in the way of self denial and virtue.

* *
*

Prayer to ask of God a Director.

Lord, who knowest all hearts, make known to me the person whom Thou hast chosen to guide me, for I am but a child, and I know not how to walk in Thy way. I know, Lord, that Thou art the way and no one can go to Thee, save by Thy grace, but I cannot find Thee if Thou thyself dost not attract me, and if Thou givest me not a guide who will lead me to Thee. Send me a guide who may discern Thy designs for my soul,—who ponders Thy words,—who loves the doctrine of Thy Church,—who will be to me a father and mother in one, and who, after the example of St. Paul, does not fear to suffer for the sanctification of souls.

Send me a guide who will dispense Thy Holy Word with prudence, who may know how to compassionate my weakness without betraying Thy interests, and who seeks but to guide me to Thee alone. And when I shall have found him, grant me the grace, O my God, to heed him, as I would heed Thee, to obey him as I would obey Thee.

CHAPTER FOURTH.

Abuse of Direction.

In this Chapter and the following, we shall treat, not only of the director, but also of the confessor, who, particularly in communities, without being properly the director of the house, gives, nevertheless, a general impetus to all souls in the same house under his direction. With still stronger reason does this Chapter apply to persons in the world, who have no other director than their confessor.

These abuses of which we have to speak may arise from :

1st. The multiplicity of directors.
2d. Changing directors.
3d. The relations with a director.

I.

Abuse arising from a multiplicity of Directors.

Unity of direction, particularly in a community, is founded :

1st. On the conduct and spirit of the

Church, which ensures communities extraordinary confessors at the four Ember seasons, and during a retreat, which requires that a superior be willing, in a few extraordinary cases, to call in a strange confessor, and requires that every religious be permitted to send for any confessor she wishes at the hour of death ; all of which regulations presuppose habitually uniform direction.

2d. On experience ; in communities where there are several directors, there is a division of sentiments and opinions, and it rarely happens that the peace of the community is not disturbed.

They speak of the confessors,—they compare them one with another,—they uphold one, they censure, or at least disapprove, of another... Thence follow rash judgments ; parties are formed which, though perhaps not compromising in the beginning, end by destroying the peace of the community. It is remarked, for example, that souls directed by such a confessor go to Holy Communion more frequently, etc. Thence follow particularly, attachments, not very deep-seated doubtless, but always inimical to a spirit of faith, and sometimes ridiculous ; thence follow prejudices, so strong, that some will miss a communion rather than go to confession to the other confessor, whom they do not like, merely because they did not begin by going to him.

3d. On reason. The director is the chief, and gives the same impetus.

He is the father, he gives the same nourishment. With one director there is but one and the same spirit;—the spirit of God does not dwell where there is a want of union.*

In the world, a multiplicity of directors has also deplorable results.

There are souls who have several directors and several confessors at the same time; they go from one to the other, sometimes in the same day, usually choosing one for the confession of grave sins, the other for sins they suppose less serious.

Poor souls, unconscious that the spirit which impels them is a spirit of pride, sometimes of hypocrisy, always a frivolous spirit at least, and that they run the risk, when there is question of confession, of profaning a sacrament, which they approach without one

---

* It is well to have but one spiritual father but that does not, as St. Francis de Sales says, prevent one from communicating with several others. St. Teresa made a vow of obedience to P. Gratien, but it did not prevent her from asking counsel.

Unity of direction, does not in any way prohibit giving confidences and making communications to another director (*Principles of Mystical Theology*)

Abuse of Direction. 89

of the most essential dispositions, humility.

Such souls will never be at peace, for the decisions they receive will rarely be the same ; not that the same principles do not guide the different directors, but because they themselves unconsciously make a different representation of the state of their soul. In these frivolous souls, who go from chapel to chapel and from confessor to confessor, impressions are so transitory that the same thought takes new shape in their imagination every hour.

They will make no progress in virtue, and will remain all their lives subject to the same faults. We can only correct a fault and acquire a virtue by continuing the same efforts, and this perseverance is impossible to them because of the different impulsions they receive, and of their inconstancy which makes them undertake, interrupt, resume the same exercises several times in the same week ; moreover, one who is ill cannot be cured when his impatience leads him constantly to change his physician.

II.

Abuse in changing Directors.

A change of director may sometimes be necessary, sometimes, simply useful.

When the desire to change seems reasonable, and continues after a certain time, in spite of our submission, and prayers offered with a pure intention for light and guidance, let us, if possible, submit our desire and the reasons for it, to a stranger whom we know to be not easily influenced, and follow his advice.

We understand that such advice cannot always be obtained ; let us beware, at least when obliged to act by ourselves, of allowing our judgment to be influenced :

1st. By a spirit of frivolity We feel a need, a wholly nervous need, to change because our director wearies us, tries us, always repeats the same thing, and is not, we think, what he formerly was to us.

2d. By vanity. Our director has wounded us, humbled us, he has administered a reproof to us, he entertains suspicions against us.—We need, we argue, some one more talented, who will not treat us quite so much like a child,—we want such a director to whom the elect, privileged souls go ;—we feel ourselves called to something higher than the monotonous life in which he lets us drag wearily on.

Alas! all these motives are doubtless not as crudely put into words as we have expressed them; but let us search well and we will frequently find them in the depth of our souls.

3d. *By sensuality.* The ordinary director ceases to please us; another, in passing, preaches and hears confessions, he delights us... "Ah! here is a man of merit! What sanctity! What amiability! He is a saint!" etc., etc.

In truth, how can God bless such motives? Once more, I repeat, sound your heart well before leaving permanently the priest who has long had the care of your soul, or before asking permission to cease going to the confessor of the community.

The most useful confessors and directors are not always those who please us most, or those who excite in us most sensible fervor; but those who make us practice solid virtues: humility, self-denial, submission to the will of God, manifested by events and by the action of creatures against us.

Then, before changing, let us know how to wait a certain time and to moderate with patience all that may be natural in our desire, to manifest to God our good will to suffer a few days longer, and to be understood by Him alone. We have asked the spiritual motives for choosing a director, we ask now the spiritual motives for leaving him.

"Be not of the number of these persons" says Guilloré, "who change easily because they are seized with shame after the confession of some grave faults, or because they are disgusted, not being directed according to their own ideas, or because they are attracted by the novelty of some director of reputation. This circumstance is gravely prejudicial to the soul, for there is nothing which tends more to maintain bad habits than this facility in changing a director; doubtless we avoid by this means the confusion of our faults, but the confusion being avoided, we fearlessly fall with impunity into the same disorders.... There must be grave reasons for changing a director whom we have carefully chosen and whom we have received as from God's hand. We should not lightly undo what God has done.

* *
*

There is not question here of a temporary change, such as a confession now and then made to another confessor,—nor of a counsel asked of a worthy person whom God sends to us,—nor of a manifestation of conscience made in words or by letter to a director whose prudence is known to us.

There are certain situations in life when we need a strange voice;—there are certain troubles which we must needs confide to one for whom we feel a particular attraction;— there are, particularly, certain faults, certain kinds of temptation which we have not the courage to discover to our ordinary confessor and for which we require some one who is perfectly unknown to us.

Even though there be no extraordinary operations in the soul, we do wisely sometimes to make a retreat under a confessor and a director other than the ordinary confessor and director.

The Church in her wisdom has decreed that several times a year an extraordinary confessor should offer his ministry to the religious upon whom the rule imposes an ordinary confessor.

The religious are not obliged to confess to him, but they must all present themselves at the tribunal of penance. The Church wishes that at the hour of death every religious should be permitted to send for any confessor she desires, and that every sister be permitted to correspond directly, either with her superior general, or with the ecclesiastical superior of the community.

There are cases where a change of director is absolutely necessary.

"We must beware," says Fenelon, "of choosing a director through complacency, or policy, or through any sensible attraction, or for any reason save to find a man of God. A choice made with human motives is capable of ruining our means of salvation. If we have been so unfortunate as to fall into this fault, the only remedy will be to break away courageously from the consequences, and put our conscience at liberty to seek elsewhere succor according to our needs."

There may be other circumstances in life which imperiously require a change of director. Let us not act too quickly, and as we said, let us do nothing without the counsel of a prudent person to whom we shall have simply represented our feelings, our desires and the motives by which we are impelled.

* *
*

Here is what the "Mystical Theology" of Schram says on the important subject of changing a director:

"Though usually it is well to confide the direction of our soul to but one person, nevertheless, we should not irrevocably attach ourselves to him; we should be sufficiently indifferent towards him to be able to do without him, to be free to consult another, and even to change him at need.

Otherwise we may have reason to fear the menace of our Saviour: "Woe to him who confideth in man!"—it would be falling into the abuse blamed by the Apostle when the faithful of his time glorified themselves, saying, one: "I indeed am of Paul," another, "I am of Apollo." "What, then, is Apollo, and what is Paul?" He answers them: "The ministers of Him whom you have believed, and they labor for Him every one as the Lord hath given."

St. Teresa, in the thirteenth Chapter of her Life, praises the holy liberty with which a secular may choose a better director than her own; she would even have a like liberty in cloisters, without injury, however, to obedience, at least for consulting other priests than the confessor.

The Life of St. Jane de Chantal retraces at great length the trouble she experienced in consequence of her vow to be directed by one director, who did not suit her.

Reason fully justifies this holy liberty. There may in fact be grave cases where it is important for us to consult another director rather than the ordinary one, and even to leave the latter.

III.

Abuse in the relations with a Director.

These relations may be vitiated by a too strong attachment, by a too pronounced dislike, or by a too absolute reserve.

1st. Attachment for the Director.

1st. Attachment for a director is not censurable when it is formed by grace,—dictated by gratitude,—inspired by merited confidence.

It gives the director the authority of a father, the soul directed the docility of a child.

Our manifest confidence in the director excites his zeal, sustains and consoles him.

The confidence given by the soul directed prepares her for the action of grace, makes her happy, and enables her to more easily bear trials.*

---

* Sister Cornuau having said to Bossuet : "If I am permitted to wish that you will always continue your care of my soul, I may have reason to fear an attachment."—The learned

Abuse of Direction. 97

2d. Reprehensible, we shall not say culpable, attachment which always interferes with the workings of grace because wholly natural, is recognized by the following marks:

We desire to be esteemed and loved by our director.

We display to him, and sometimes with a refinement of humility which is pitiable, all the good qualities we recognize in ourselves, particularly exterior qualities. We tell him more or less openly that we are very much attached to him, and know not what we would do without him.

We accuse him, at least to ourselves, of partiality towards others... we would be the sole object of his interest; we speak when seeking direction, or during confession, of things proper to nourish vanity or sensuality.

We are interminable in our relations to him.

We are disquieted, disconsolate, if absence

---

prelate replied: " You cannot too earnestly desire the care of a pastor... As to too great attachments for directors, we must treat these things as we do other trials, that is, let them pass, and draw into ourselves. It is only the inevitable dust and rust to be found on faces, and the cleanest vessels; so that we must continually purify ourselves and suffer God to put us back into the fire. Here is the only remedy for this evil; every other aggravates rather than cures it.

or illness interfere with our confession, and we miss communion because we have not been able to make our confession to him; We go, without his knowledge, when the director is also the confessor, to a strange priest, to confess a humiliating fault, which will lessen,—(we imagine)—the esteem we believe merited.*

And if the confessor be changed†.. We have not here to depict scenes which would be ridiculous if truly represented, we merely wish to indicate the marks of a too natural attachment which God does not bless.

If your director be changed, remember that God remains to you.

If the instrument through which God communicated with you be broken, resources are never lacking to this All-powerful Artisan.

If the stream which conveyed God's grace to you be dry, the Source remains.

---

* We are right, certainly, to seek another priest for the confession of a grave sin, which we would perhaps confess badly to the ordinary confessor. This is not what we censure. Alas! we know how to allow for human weakness! We censure the little spirit of faith we bring to our ordinary confessions."

† The abuse of not changing a confessor when we think it necessary, is more pernicious than the contrary abuse.

Frequently changing one's director without necessity may be prejudicial to perfection, but not to change one's confessor at the risk of making bad confessions, is an abuse which may lead to perdition.

And who can say whether this change of director be not a punishment for your too natural attachment, and the feeble manner in which you profited by his words? Who can say whether God had not needs send him to other souls who will better profit by his experience?

Say not: this director is necessary to my perfection, say he is useful; God alone is necessary.

This minister was sent you by God to do you a certain good, determined by the Divine Wisdom; his mission ended, God sends him to another soul. Who was more useful to Tobias than Raphael? Raphael leaves him after his mission is accomplished.

Who was more useful for the conversion of the Chinese than St. Francis Xavier? Yet this servant of God died before setting foot in the kingdom of China.

Who was more necessary to the Apostles than our Lord? Nevertheless our Saviour declared to them that His presence was an obstacle to the coming of the Holy Ghost.

A natural attachment for one's director is one of the great obstacles to the operations of grace, and never will a soul that yields to the sweetness of this affection, however innocent it may be, attain the degree of perfection to which God calls her.

Listen to this remarkable page from the *Memoirs* of M. Ollier : " It pleased our Lord to show me one thing upon which I must instruct and enlighten souls who come to me ; that is, turn them from certain practices in which they indulge, innocently, though they are far removed from the purity of God, who desires souls perfectly detached, dead to themselves, and everywhere void of all created things. For example, they affect to receive communion at the mass of their confessors and directors ; this deprives them of much grace, weakens God's operations and His pleasure in them.

" A person who goes to hear the mass of a priest for whom she feels a particular friendship or esteem, however holy it may be, must necessarily risk turning to him from time to time with certain complacent, pleasurable feelings, certain interior satisfaction, which incline her to rest, to lean upon, and delight in what is human, earthly, created, which is not God alone, and His purity, which nevertheless must form the sole object of the soul's aspirations

" All that leads us to turn the eyes of our soul from God, and to fix them upon the

Abuse of Direction. 101

creature, is a temptation, a distraction, odious to God, particularly in holy things like sacrifice and prayer."*

2nd. *Dislike for one's Director.*

A dislike for a director arises, we have already said, from wounded self love, a frustrated illusion, or a prejudice.

We have not found in his direction what we expected;—we imagine that he is no longer the same to us, and this thought increasing, closes our heart.—Hence we approach him with hesitation, we speak with embarrassment, we reply with visible fear, often in terms that are scarcely polite, and necessarily we find, or imagine, that he re-

---

*" I cannot " writes an experienced soul, "resist calling your attention to the ridiculousness of two kinds of persons. There are some who have one appointed director and several others in reserve. Excuse the two expressions ; alas ! they are too sadly true ! Others go to the other extreme. They have but one director, but he is so unique that no other priest is of any value in their eyes. And if this wounderful director goes away they are inconsolable ; the whole city knows the terrible loss they have sustained and how impossible it is for them to go to any other priest.

"Avoid the inconstancy of the first and the exclusiveness of the second. Keep your director as long as God leaves him to you. In case of absence or departure, be resigned, pray and with the assistance of God's grace, go to another. Let your attitude towards your director be a supernatural one. The priest is Jesus Christ. Your director is in a measure Jesus Christ adapting Himself to you, to better purify, enlighten, strengthen and console you. Never forget this great truth, and know how to observe a happy medium between pusillanimity and familiarity."

ceives us coldly, is short in his words, severe in his decisions.... and we plan a change which, if not possible, pre-occupies us, disquiets us and completely destroys our peace.

Dislike for the ordinary director may arise from very different causes :

There are dispositions which love change, and tire of the best things ; they must have novelty.

Others want a confessor, who talks a great deal in the confessional, and gives them long sermons.

Others want some one with whom they may discuss everything both in and out of confession. A solid man who says little and to the point dissatisfies them.

There are persons who seek a confessor who follows their tastes and inclinations ; who flatters them, spares them, who conforms himself to their ideas of spirituality, who authorizes all their judgments, and all they wish, as if the approbation they receive justified their immortification. Poor deluded souls, who seek in the condescension and indulgence of their directors what may maintain their negligence and not the remedy for the evil.

Sometimes dislike for a director and con-

Abuse of Direction. 103

sequently a desire to leave him, comes from jealousy. We would like to be of a limited number, and we are not; we imagine that the director has more consideration for others, that he gives them more time, as if a priest had not to give himself to each soul according to its need!

There are some, finally, who tire of a director who knows how to control them, who wishes them to advance in virtue, who excites and urges them on. They would rather give up everything than subject themselves to reproaches and urgent solicitations.

O! the pitiable devotion of such souls! How ill it is understood, how puerile, or rather, how dangerous it is! Dislike for a confessor and director may sometimes be the effect of the devil's malice, who, wishing to hinder the good which certain direction effects in a soul, fills her with a vague disquiet, groundless suspicion, an almost unconquerable weariness.

This dislike also arises simply by the permission of God, who would oblige a soul to act with more purity of intention and to seek only God in the director.

Whatever the source of this dislike, a spirit of faith, humility, and patient submission are the means by which we may dissipate it or render it meritorious.

What soul, in fact, convinced that she has no right after all her infidelities to the fatherly care of God, will not esteem herself fortunate that God deigns to concern Himself for her, even though He permits His orders and counsels to be transmitted to her in a way which is irritating to her sensitiveness, and displeasing to her nature?

3rd. *Reserve with the Director.*

This reserve which, in the beginning, may be only the result of timidity and which in this case gradually disappears, is more frequently the fruit of self love or prejudice, and always a want of a spirit of faith.

It prevents the director, the spiritual physician, from learning and consequently curing your infirmities by applying suitable remedies.

It prevents the director, the guide of your soul, from leading you to the degree of perfection which God requires of you, for it is necessary that this guide know the lights with which you have been favored, the causes of your imperfections, the nature of your temperament.

Here, in the words of an experienced director, is practically what this reserve leads to, which prevents you from discovering the depths of your soul.

" This reserve may be observed concerning evil inclinations, or graces and gifts of God."

1st. You who only mention in a general way, or scarce make any mention of your evil inclinations, who fear that their source may be found, and all their results discovered, and particularly that your affection for them may be revealed, —do you know the result of this want of frankness?

Ever in a state of tepidity and imperfection, you will always continue slothful and imperfect. In a state of degeneracy and decline, you will gradually weaken day by day, and perhaps you will be the only one to whom it will not be apparent. In a state of trial and temptation you will be without support and you will be overcome; or your soul disquieted and tormented, without bearing the stain of sin will experience all its trouble and bitterness. In a state of doubt and perplexity, you will not act, and you will leave a virtuous act undone; or you will act against the light of your conscience and you will make a false step, which will bring disorder into your life.

You who in a general or ordinary confession will have concealed a weakness which it still costs you an effort to confess, do you know what will be the consequences of this reticence? You will groan under the habitual slavery of sin. You will approach the sacraments and you will profane them. Your life will be but a series of faults and remorse. Fortunate, if awakened by the cries of conscience, you cast yourself into the arms of God and His minister to procure for yourself, by a faithful confession, the consolations which religion offers you.

You, finally, who with habitual faults, of which every one complains, and for which you have so often been reproved, whether a frivolous spirit of dissipation, a hard capricious disposition, a proud and haughty humor, or a tendency to taunt and contradict your sisters,—carelessly and superficially expose these dispositions to your confessor, do you know what will be the result? Your passions always immortified, will prevent any change being visible in your conduct, and will follow you perhaps to the tomb. Your communions will be as useless as they are frequent, and the little fruit you derive from them will be a source of regret to your confessor, or bitter grief to your superior,

Abuse of Direction. 107

and of bad example to the community.

We do not sufficiently expose the depths of our soul to God's minister, because we hold to our passions, and disguise our faults from ourselves. That sister, for example, who wearies the others by her obstinacy, her sudden sallies of impatience, her bruskness, finds reasons to excuse and sometimes to even justify herself. And with such dispositions, how does she accuse herself? I accuse myself of impatience she will say, and confine herself to this short accusation. The spiritual father finding it insufficient, questions her to learn the nature of the fault. Was it a sudden movement of impatience which escaped you? Did you indulge it? Was it accompanied with unkind words which pained another? "My daughter," continues the confessor, "it is only a sally of impatience, but you fall into this fault repeatedly, you do not correct it; but you must overcome yourself." —"It is true," answers the penitent, "I wish I could do better; but I am weak, I was born with this tendency; it carries me away. To be silent and gentle upon certain occasions would require the virtue of an angel."
—Thus instead of accusing, she seeks to justify herself with apologies, or to make only half accusations; and after such imperfect

accusations what do we see? the same passions, the same faults, the same habits.

Another sister accuses herself of disputing with a companion engaged in the same work. What is the reason of it? An antipathy which she will not overcome, too great attachment to her own ideas, pride wounded by a word, a contradiction, a reproach; but all this is suppressed, there is no mention of these various motives. The director suspects some reticence on the part of the interested person. The very vehemence with which she expresses herself makes him feel that he must distrust her representations. He enters into detail, he asks questions, he administers a reproof, how is it received? "Ah! Father you blame me, you will not hear me. If you knew all I have to suffer, and how difficult it is to live with certain characters!" A moment after, the sister, the subject of complaint, comes and relates the same fact, and in a more temperate manner cites a circumstance which betrays the historian, and develops the mystery. Is this confessing one's sins and seeking direction? Is it not rather convincing a director of what he already knows and what experience teaches us, that your sex has a singular skill in dressing a fact to favor its weakness and in devoutly deceiving with an air of truthfulness?

What! from this wise and wholesomely severe hand which is to cure your wounds by the application of the lancet and caustic, you seek a false condescension which flatters and caresses them!

Another sister accuses herself of having failed in respect to her mistress or her superior. Represent to her that respect towards superiors is a rigorous obligation, that all who govern are the depositories of the power and authority of God Himself, that He receives in their person the homage of submission or the insult of revolt, she excuses, palliates the fault which is only too evident:—"I do not like that mistress; she does not attract me; that superior does not inspire me with sufficient confidence, and she may be mistaken."—Thus after failing in obedience and submission, she goes to confession and in the very tribunal where she should repair her fault, she adds another, a want of humility and compunction.

Such is the usual cause of the little fruit produced by the sacraments and of so many useless, sometimes sacrilegious confessions and communions. They content themselves with a superficial exposition, without discovering the depths and the condition of the soul. They declare to the priest a few exterior faults, they show him, if I may so speak, a few reptiles from the human heart, but without giving him the key of the abyss.

2d. We sin also against direction through reserve, by not being sufficiently open concerning the graces and gifts received from God. These gifts should be examined, respected and made profitable.

First, they should be examined. The Apostle St. John forbids us to believe every spirit, but tells us to try them.* These gifts of God, and these special attractions of which I speak, must then be submitted, for our security, to examination, in order not to confound divine operations with the work of the imagination and the illusions of the spirit of darkness. To what false lights, to what illusions and errors we expose ourselves! and how many souls are deceived because they will walk alone without a guide!

Secondly, these gifts should be respected. It is respecting them, to communicate them when God inspires us to. It is respecting them, to seek in this communication a means of exciting ourselves to the needful gratitude

---
* John iv.

for them, learning to believe ourselves unworthy of them, and detaching ourselves from that self examination and vain complacency which are the shoal in such favors.

Thirdly, they must bear fruit. In fact, God never bestows a grace with the intention of giving but one. The first which we receive is a fruitful germ of those which follow, and God, master of His gifts and anxious to distribute them, waits only our co-operation to multiply them.

This co-operation requires continuous efforts which only a director can help us to make; it requires lights which God, to preserve us in humility, usually gives to others to be communicated to us.

It is thus, pious souls, by exposing your conscience, and opening your heart with simplicity that you will walk in the way God has traced for you, and attain the perfection He requires of you; while with your reserve and your false timidity you will remain always imperfect, and oblige God to withdraw His graces from you.

CHAPTER FIFTH.

Duties of the soul directed.

As this work is written particularly for souls under direction, we shall not speak of the duties of the director.

We have just said a word of the spirit of faith, without which direction becomes, to a large number of souls, an insupportable tyranny, a source of vexation, murmurs, trials . . . we shall confine ourselves to this.

The soul under direction must :

1st. Pray much for her Director.

This is a duty of gratitude and personal interest.

1st. We shall not dwell upon the director's necessary devotion,—upon the vexations he must conquer,—upon the repugnances he must overcome,—the time he must sacrifice, —the fatigue he must endure,—the little consolation he receives,—the ingratitude he sometimes encounters . . . . all things which require on his part courage, energy, self denial, charity. He is much to be pitied if he has not the glory of God in view, if he is not sustained by this thought : I am sanctifying myself,—I am performing an act of charity,— I am taking God's place

And you, the object of his care, must be very selfish and unfeeling, if you have not some gratitude for one whom you find ever ready to hear you and to help you; if you have not a little patience with one who is so patient with you, who sometimes is already wearied and tired for hours when you come to fatigue him still more, and who asks of you no pecuniary compensation, not even thanks or affection but only a few prayers for his soul.

2d. Your own interest requires that you pray for your director. What, in fact, do you desire? To become virtuous and sanctify yourself?... to do this you need the counsel, the help, the protection of a person who has few human resources, and who, outside of faith, finds nothing to sustain him in his ministry.

Then ask for your director, abundant light, that he may clearly see your needs, and the means he must adopt to meet them.

Ask for him wisdom, that he may not require what is above your strength, and that he may neither lighten nor increase the burden which God gives you to bear.

Ask for him kindness, that he may not repel you, that he may treat you with patience, affection, in a spirit of God.

Ask for him sanctity, that he may have no other object but to lead you to God, and that he may sanctify himself in doing you good.

Pray every day for him, pray especially the day you are going to him.

2d. The soul under direction must seriously will to become better.

This is the end of direction; and if your will be very firm in this respect, you will be happy to seek direction, or you will at least seek it with the thought, a sufficiently stimulating one: that you are going to gain strength thereby.

This firm will, will cause you to overcome the repugnance you may feel from time to time, and which may arise from a vague weariness for which you cannot account.

It will cause you to despise the humiliation you will necessarily feel in exposing your miseries, and at finding yourself always with the same imperfections and faults.

It will cause you to observe the practice of seeking direction as assiduously as you do that of confession.

It will render you simple and docile, to adopt at once the method of prayer, or plan of conduct, suggested to you, to abandon without regret the practices of piety to which you are accustomed,—to will, in a word, all that he wills who takes God's place to you.

A soul of good will acts when she is told to act, abstains from action when told to abstain, withdraws at the first word from anything which she has imprudently or inconsiderately undertaken. She makes, unmakes, interrupts, resumes, labors anew, multiplies her efforts, rests, mortifies herself according to the counsel of him who guides her.

3d. A soul under direction must be simple.

" The sisters' simple and childlike confidence in their Mother, will fill Paradise with religious," said St. Chantal.

" Have a heart of crystal, fear only one thing, not being thoroughly known to your director. ' How I wish,' says P. Lallemant, ' I could take my interior between my hands and show it just as it is !' "

If you see only God in your director, you will be simple, frankly answering the questions which are put to you,— accepting without murmur the reproaches you receive, yen when little merited,—suffering no doubt, and even keenly, at finding yourself suspected, perhaps misunderstood, but recognizing it only as a trial, or permitted by God to humble you.

If you are simple, you will tell your efforts, your combats, your falls, your successes;— you will make known your plans with a fixed resolution to pursue them or abandon them according as you are counselled,—finally you will heartily and affectionately thank your guide and return to your daily life.

"Every month, the sisters" writes St. Francis de Sales "shall briefly and summarily expose their heart to the superior in all simplicity, and with faithful confidence show her its innermost depths with the same sincerity and candor that a child would show its scratches and bruises to its mother, and by this means they will render an account as much of their advancement and progress, as of their losses and failings in exercises, and prayer, in virtues and the interior life, manifesting also their interior and exterior temptations, not only to seek consolation, but to be strengthened and humbled.

"Happy those who practice with frank

simplicity this article of the constitutions which teaches a portion of that holy spiritual infancy which our Lord has recommended so much and which creates and maintains true tranquillity of spirit."

Simplicity gently opens the soul without any reserve whatever, and does not fear that the director may see too clearly.

Does she fear to make known her weaknesses? but she wishes to correct them and she knows that her efforts will be more apparent to her director than her miseries;—her faults? but she is sincerely sorry for them and she knows that this sorrow will cause her cowardice to be forgotten;—her desires? her projects? but she admits none that God's eye could find reprehensible. If some of them claim her attention, she reveals them with great frankness, and states the impression they make upon her, ready to energetically reject them, the moment her confessor shall say: "This desire, this project will profit you nothing!"

When we act thus, God does not permit us to be deceived or even our soul to be disquieted.

Duties of the soul directed.

4th. A soul under direction must be obedient.

Obedience to a director is a consequence of the spirit of faith.

When St. Paul went to the early faithful of Galatia, he was received as an angel and as Jesus Christ Himself. "And with reason," says St. Thomas, "for it was really Jesus Christ who came to them, hidden under the exterior of this great Saint."

Our director is an Angel expressly sent us by God to make known His will to us.

"And if he is a priest," says St. Bonaventure, "he is another Jesus Christ, for where, think you, Jesus Christ to be?" adds the Saint. "In the breast of a good priest, and in the heart of a wise director."

We must approach him then with a heart disposed to receive as an oracle all that he will say in relation to our soul.

Therefore, faithful, absolute, unreserved obedience to him. Obedience without examination, discussion or equivocation, to all that he commands, short of what is contrary to the commandments of God, the Church or the rule. Represent to him, doubtless, any undesirable result which you think may follow from what he commands, but if he insists, always submit and obey.*

Obedience in regard to the modifications in the commandments of the Church and some points of the rule, which he thinks right to command, particularly, if the director be our superior—in regard to superfluities which he thinks right to retrench in our dress, our furniture, or any of those thousand and one things to which the heart becomes attached,—in regard to the *labor* he thinks useful for us to perform, and even the manner of performing it.

In a word, faithful, blind, prompt, generous obedience.

"In regard to the particular guidance of the soul," says St. Francis de Sales, "it must obey the special director and confessor; search as you will, says the devout Avila, you will never so assuredly find the will of God as by this path of humble obedience so recommended and practised by the early Saints.

---

* "If the director is mistaken," says P. Grou, "no harm will result to you who obey with a spirit of faith. God will bless your submission and obedience. He will prevent or repair the evil consequences of this error. God never abandons a soul that obeys for love of Him; He is pledged to this by His Providence, since He wishes that in the priest who represents Him, we behold Himself.

"We must believe directors and spiritual physicians, for God, who loves obedience, often renders useful the counsel we accept from another, and particularly from directors of souls, though there be otherwise no reason for following it ; just as He rendered the water of the Jordan profitable to Naaman, which Elias, without any apparent human reason, had commanded him to use.

"You should work out your interior good by the means judged suitable by those appointed to guide souls.—We would be taught perhaps and instructed by God Himself in the way of ecstacies, raptures and visions, and I know not what similar foolishness, manufactured in our imagination, rather than follow the salutary and common way of holy submission to those whom God has sent us. Now, though it is very certain that God will work miracles rather than leave unaided, either spiritually or temporally, those who fully trust themselves to His care and Providence, He wishes nevertheless that we should do on our part all that lies in our power ; that is, He wills that we should make use of the ordinary means of perfection, in default of which, He will never fail to help us. But while His will is signified to us, and we have persons who tell us what we must do, let us not expect that God will work miracles to teach us and lead us to perfection, for He will not.

" Let your spiritual director command the pious actions you should perform, for they will be better, and will have double grace and merit : merit in themselves that they are pious, and the merit of obedience which commands them and in virtue of which they are done."

* *
*

Remember, however, that this obedience must leave your soul in peace, and permit you to act without scruple, according to circumstances, notwithstanding the counsel you have received, when it is not apparent that you can do otherwise.

Only render an account, when you next seek direction, of the course you pursued and the reasons you had for so doing.

Counsels for the practice of virtue may be excellent in themselves, yet, when the time comes to apply them, we may find that we can only do so with great difficulty, or at the risk of grave consequences which could not have been foreseen.

It is different when the application of the

counsel is absolutely necessary to avoid sin.

"A spiritual director," says Father Faber, "is not a monastic superior. Our obedience to the last, must be minute; to the first, general.

"The superior's jurisdiction is universal, the director's only where we invite it, or he asks it and we accord it.

"The superior turns into precepts matters of supererogation; a director must have forgotten himself if he attempts anything of the kind.

"If we disobey a superior, we sin; it would require very peculiar and unusual circumstances to make disobedience to our director any sin at all."

Let us beware particularly of making a vow of obedience to our director, even if he is also our confessor. A few Saints have doubtless made this vow with profit to their souls, but it was under special and rare circumstances, and then, they lived a life of such intimate union with God, in such perfect detachment from creatures, in such continual mortification of their senses and desires, in such profound humility, and God led them by such extraordinary ways, that their example can in no way be a rule to us. Grave inconvenience may result from this vow of obedience made in a moment of fervor.

5th. The soul under direction must be discreet.

To speak little of one's director is great wisdom;—to extol him upon all occasions is great imprudence.

Some speak of him through vanity. The director is learned, he directs a great many, and we are very glad to have it known that we have been accepted as his penitent, and that under his direction, one becomes a great saint.

Others speak of him through extravagant affection, which, if not guilty, is at least ill regulated and they are sometimes the cause of much annoyance to their directors, who for the most part are wholly unconscious of the attachment they have inspired.

Others speak through pure heedlessness, and a desire to talk, telling without reflection the questions they submitted to him, his replies, the counsels they received, the decisions they obtained, . . . they repeat these decisions, these counsels, in their own incomplete, imperfect way, and put in the mouth of the director, a multitude of things which he never said....

Others speak to complain, particularly when the director is appointed, and they are not free to leave him... These over delicate souls, habitually filled with themselves, do not see that the complaints in which they indulge,—even though not without foundation, will awaken in other trusting, happy souls, suspicions, fears, and vague disquiet, and from that moment weaken their confidence.... How responsible before God, is one who censures a director! What an account he will have to render for having paralyzed the good which an authorized director could have effected in a religious house!

When a soul feels a desire to complain of her director, it is pretty certain she is not united to God....Ah! dear soul, at times when you find your director less kind, less patient, or he seems to pay no more attention to you, instead of murmuring and imparting with exaggeration your impressions to others, go before our dear Lord and humbly acknowledge that there must be a secret evil within you which God wills to cure with a little harshness.

Sometimes, no doubt, the director wishes to satisfy himself of the soul's strength, but very often he is only God's instrument for you. God gives to the tone of his voice a harshness of which he is not conscious, places on his lips an expression which has wounded you and which it was not his intention to use to you—your complaint is not against him alone, but reflects upon God.

Remember that his manner of guiding you whatever it may be, will always be profitable if you accept it as coming from God.

Be also discreet in communicating to others the counsels you have received from your director.

" Have you," says a pious work, " well reflected on the character of intimacy and even individuality which characterise confession and direction ? Only the priest and your soul ! The priest thinks only of Jesus Christ and your soul. You on your part have to think but of Jesus Christ and your soul. My secret is mine, mine is my secret ; practice these words of Holy Scripture. That which is for you, must not be applied to others, and as a general rule cannot be applied to them.

"When God has caused a thought or word to reach you which touches your heart, keep it there. If the person to whom you communicate it be not moved by it, she may take it in a contrary sense, and thus thwart God's designs.

"When we decide to communicate something which has passed between the director and the soul, it must be with the intention to increase in certain persons their love for Our Lord, their confidence in the guidance of Providence, or to help them in a difficult or painful situation ; for example, to overcome a temptation which we have experienced and for which we have been shown a remedy.

"Outside of these exceptional and necessarily rare cases, keep for your soul alone the words with which God has inspired your director for your soul alone.

"Imitate the Blessed Virgin who carefully preserved in her heart the great things she saw and heard."

6th. A soul under direction must be humble.

The more humble the soul is, the more real and even sensible will be the profit she derives from direction.

More humility is perhaps required in seeking direction than in the practice of confession, either because we must expose with more detail than confession requires, our want of firmness, our inconstancy, our bad will,—or particularly, because a director must treat us with less consideration than a confessor.

He must form us to virtue, and he can only do so by causing us to practice self-denial, and self-denial is not learned so much by mortifying ourselves as by letting others mortify us. The director then must go counter to our desires by restraining us when we wish to go forward, by forbidding us austerities which we would like to practice, and even extra communions which we are led to ask,—by giving us scarcely a word when we expected a long conference,—by meeting a confident outpouring of our heart with a few dry, brief words, by requiring such a practice which tries us, such an act of submission or charity at which our self-love revolts.

How, upon these occasions, and so many others which God contrives with us, are we to continue confident, submissive, respectful, without a great depth of humility?

To how many souls a less cordial reception, a want of time, which prevented a director from hearing them as long as they wished, a harsh word designedly spoken sometimes to try them, have been sufficient to rouse them against their director and cause them to leave him in search of some one, they tell you, who better understands them, consoles them more affectionately, and is more advanced in the ways of God.

Poor souls, poor souls, if you were more humble, that is, convinced that because of your sins you did not deserve that God should give you a director who occupies himself specially with you,—that in hearing you he performs a great act of charity,— that you ought to be very happy to be able to reach heaven by suffering, by being thought ill of, rebuffed, misunderstood, how grateful you would be to this good priest, and this good superior, who, in hearing you, spend time which they both might employ more usefully for themselves; how submissive and patient you would be; how carefully you would gather the least of their counsels, how earnestly you would thank them, and how fervently you would pray for them!

Be humble, be humble, ask God to make you very humble!

"There are no good directors," say certain persons impelled by a secret pride to pose as elect souls.

"It is not true," Bourdaloue answers, "there are many directors, but few persons who allow themselves to be directed.

"Not that all, or nearly all, devout persons do not wish to have a director, but a director after their own fashion, who directs them according to their ideas, a director whom they themselves direct as to how they must be directed.

"This is not wishing a director but wishing to direct one's self through a director."

"There are certain devotees," says Fr. Crasset, "who affect to be unable to find a director to their taste. They must change every month, and to justify their fickleness cite the example of St. Teresa, whom the greater number of directors were unable to direct, and St. Francis de Sales, who says, a director must be one chosen among a thousand.

"I acknowledge St. Teresa needed learned and experienced directors, but are you a St. Teresa? Do you obey all your confessors as she did? Do you do all they command, even to leaving, when obedience ordered, our Lord who visibly appeared to her?

"If, like her, you are humble, docile, and obedient, the Son of God will not fail to send you when the proper time arrives, men more capable and enlightened than your confessors. Meanwhile He will instruct you Himself, without, however, dispensing you from the obedience you owe them.

"Persons who are so fastidious in the matter of directors, and so difficult to please probably need one to teach them the elements of the spiritual life, which are humility and mortification." *

7th. A Summary.

Ancient writers have expressed in the following axioms the sum of one's actions in relation to a director :

Consule—to consult   *Carpe*—to accept.
Solare —to calm.   *Doce* —to learn.
Remitte —to pardon. *Fer* —to endure.
Ora—to pray.

—*Consult*, ask advice instead of following

---

* The false devotee is indocile to direction though she affect to be under the direction of the most clever and enlightened. After much peregrination, you believe her settled and definitely submissive to direction ; no such thing. Her plan is made in advance, her life is mapped out, her practices labelled, nothing must be changed. She is prodigal in protestations of submission, but at the least word of contradiction she rebels, murmurs, protests, poses as misunderstood. For example attempt to introduce some order into her numerous practices. It is a sacrilegious interference. Refuse her a communion which she asks ! It is treating her with barbarity.

If she have a mania for representing herself as very unworthy, a mania which is often but a shade of pride, or a refuge of cowardice, and you endeavor to dispose her to receive the grace of the sacraments, you are hardening her, brutalizing her.

Or, if she assents to all your counsels and commands, it is to have her own way under pretexts which she is in the habit of finding perfectly reasonable.

Thwarted in her caprices and fancies, or to speak more elegantly, in her religious autonomy, she endeavors to find a good-natured, weak man, whom she can adroitly bend to her will, and if she succeeds, she will be convinced that at last she has the proper kind of direction.—*Or et alliage.*

your inspirations which are rarely disinterested, or may be the perfidious flatteries of false friends who have the weakness to abandon you to the mercy of your caprices.

—*Accept.* Accept reproof with humility, and correction without murmur, complaint, or resentment, if you would not weary and discourage the kind charity of your guide.

—*Calm* yourself : Direction is a soothing balm, a vivifying dew, a mingling of wine and oil which nourish the soul. Show your wounds, let the physician do as he wills, suffer him to see them and simply accept the compassion he shows you.

—*Pardon* any pain he may cause you in touching your wounds, just as your physician himself must pardon the vagaries of your sick soul.

—*Endure.* No one is free from faults ; your director, alas ! has his, as you have yours ; bear with them, forget them as he bears with and forgets yours.

—*Pray.* Finally, pray God to give your guide the special wisdom he needs, which he himself also asks for, that he may be more useful to you ; pray God to make you docile that you may profit by the great favor He bestows upon you in giving you a director.

8th. A few counsels.

Let your conversations with your director be neither too long, nor filled with news or irrelevant matters.

After treating of the affairs of your soul, withdraw. " Little incidents, natural affections, glide therein so easily," says Guilloré, " that if we are not careful, we degenerate after a few words upon God, into a hundred idle remarks. Then do not remain too long with your director ; necessary things do not require hours to settle them."

Beware, as we have already said, of attaching yourself to him too sensibly, let there always be more respect than affection between you ; God withdraws from a soul whose memory is filled with the thought of a creature, however holy he may be.

Never speak to him in unusual places ; see him as a priest in the confessional rather than at his house. In the confessional you can better treat of the affairs of your soul ; your conversation is more serious and more free from all that may be human, it is easier to open your heart, and God's blessing is more abundant.

Do not let caprice regulate the days for seeking direction. In communities, the time for it is fixed by the rule, and we have not to concern ourselves to do it ; it is the director moreover who determines the time, and we must abide by his decision except in extraordinary cases.

The heart of a superior and a priest is always open to receive those who need him.

CHAPTER SIXTH.

Objections to the practice of Direction.

No one denies the usefulness and advantages of direction in general, but when there is question of putting it in practice, many pious persons raise a multitude of objections, which we shall answer after first showing the source from which they arise.

Sources of these objections.

1st. Self love, which is unwilling to expose its miseries, and acknowledge its faults, which particularly finds it onerous to seek sanction in those thousand details of the interior life, which, after all, concern, it tells you, only God and the soul.

Nature at all times has rebelled against absolute submission, but we may say that the spirit of independence has never so generally possessed souls as at the present day.

Who does not see it, who does not feel it even in the most pious houses? Who even in comparing the present state of his soul with that of fifteen years ago, does not find more revolt against authority than formerly?

Should not this be a stronger reason for forcing one's self to that exposition of the heart which subjugates and humbles us?

2d. A spirit of self sufficiency, a necessary consequence of self love, which leads proud souls to believe that they know all they are to hear, that they have no need of the counsel they are told to seek, that they could give it equally as well as the person appointed to impart it; finally, that they are not children to be led step by step, with no power to act for themselves.

3d. Sloth and sensuality, which find it hard to thus expose one's weaknesses which, after all, are effaced by the sacrament of Penance; that the yoke of confession is sufficiently painful without submitting to another yoke no less humiliating.

4th. The jealousy of the evil one, who knows that a soul under the protection of her director is fortified by his counsels, is safe against his attacks, and cannot be either overcome by his efforts, or surprised by his snares, who understands that a soul without a director is accessible to all kinds of illusions, that she is a city without ramparts,—that he may approach her, and penetrate her with all the most extravagant delusions; he will furnish a thousand reasons, a thousand pretexts, a thousand inventions, a thousand chimeras, a thousand phantoms to persuade her not to submit to direction.

Answers to the principal objections to direction, particularly in communities.

1st. *My director is not a priest: now only a priest has the necessary grace for direction.*

You forget first of all that there is no question of receiving absolution. Nor is your superior a priest, and yet you obey him because he is vested with an authority which comes from God. If, as a religious, your rule tells you to go to him for direction, he will have special light from heaven to guide you.

Moreover, it is not as a criminal that you unveil your soul, but as an imperfect soul; nor is it making a confession, but simply opening your heart; you do not exactly seek theological decisions, but instruction and counsel upon the manner of observing your rule, of correcting a fault, of overcoming a prejudice, and which a superior can give as profitably as a director.

Neither St. Francis of Assisi nor St.

Francis of Paul were priests, yet they were wise and renowned directors.

Neither St. Teresa nor St. Chantal were priests, and yet do you think that their knowledge of the things of God would not be sufficient to direct your soul?

2d. *But if my director and my superior are neither of them Saints like these?*

Who told you they are not? At the time when these directors I have just mentioned lived, St. Francis of Assisi was treated as a fool, as an ignorant, weak mind by some of his brothers.

St. Teresa was called a visionary and even said to be one of the Illuminati* by some of her sisters.

Would you be of the number of those poor religious?

St. Francis of Assisi had his faults, and St. Teresa had hers. " She was considered a woman of no judgment, and the religious of the monastery of the Incarnation went so far as to say that she ought to be shut up in prison."

Let us not go outside of a spirit of faith

---

*A sect, condemned by the Inquisition, which taught that there was no need of a spiritual director, but that each soul was to trust to what he believes to be the sacred inspirations of the Holy Ghost and to follow them at all hazards.

in reasoning upon direction. All the objections you make reflect upon the obedience due to your superior.

3d. *My director is very young, and at my age it is very trying to ask counsel of one so young.*

We shall answer this by a few lines written by St. Augustine to the Bishop Auxilien. "Behold me, an old man, ready to listen to the counsels of a young bishop; I, who have been a bishop so many years, accept the advice of a colleague who can hardly count a year of episcopacy."

We shall answer still better by the words of Jesus Christ: "Unless you be converted and become as little children you shall not enter into the kingdom of heaven."

We have recalled the example of Jesus Christ questioning and listening in the temple to the Doctors of the law; we could cite excellent examples of the submission respect and deference manifested to young superiors by old religious who had formerly been superiors themselves. "In the religious state," says one of the early masters, "there is no one, whatever his years, so ignorant as to think it unbecoming his age to practice obedience, a virtue which God Himself held it no dishonor to practice. The exercise of humility and obedience is necessary to youth, but to old age it is honorable, it is its glory and its crown."

What is human knowledge, wisdom, and experience compared to the knowledge, wisdom and experience of God? Now God has sent His spirit to your superior to guide you to heaven.

"The seniors," says St. Thomas, "must receive lessons in certain respects, because in all matters relating to prudence no one is sufficient for himself."

4th. *When I go for direction I find nothing to say.*

Then you are a great Saint since there is nothing to reform in you; not even a degree to be added to your virtues! Is that your idea? Truly we would not venture to believe you possessed of so much pride.

St. Francis de Sales, St. Teresa, St. Francis Xavier, St. Vincent of Paul, always found something wherewith to reproach themselves, and you can find nothing!

Alas! may it not be that you fear to find, or *rather*, that another will find something.

However, in the next Chapter we will

state at some length for your benefit, the subjects which form matter of direction.

5th. *I wish to speak but I cannot. I feel my heart is closed.*

This, it must be acknowledged, is the greatest obstacle to direction when we seek it with the proper dispositions.

When the heart is closed it is indeed hard to come before a superior who waits for you to speak, who may imagine perhaps that you are unwilling to speak, that you fear him, that you have no confidence in his light.

Poor soul, I pity you, and yet I would say to you : When the time for direction comes, go to your superior, but go first before the Blessed Sacrament for a moment and say fervently :

"My God, open my heart and my lips. Accept in expiation of my ill-made confessions these few moments which will be so painful to me."

Then go with all simplicity, answer the questions which are put to you; at the end, if it be the custom, ask your superior's blessing and withdraw, satisfied that you have fulfilled a duty.

This reticence is sometimes a temptation

of the evil one, and this temptation is usually dissipated by making it known to the director ; it requires but a slight effort to say : " I have a fear of you to day, " and these words will put you both at ease.

It is sometimes a trial on the part of God, but it is only temporary, and passes after a time of patience and humility.

It is sometimes a punishment of our too natural affection for this same director, or another person. God wishes us to be detached; let us profit by the lesson He gives us, and permit not our heart to rest in that of another.

It may be the result of a delicate nervous state of health, or of a feeling of prejudice in consequence of a reproof, or of an uncharitable remark some one has made about the director.

Let us pray, let us wait, let us suffer, and do our duty. Let us have the frankness to say when we seek direction: " Mother, have the kindness to question me, I will answer as well as I can."

6th. *My Director is not discreet.*

Are you very sure ? If what you have told him is known, are you certain it was he who repeated it, and that you did not give your confidence to any one else? Or if he really spoke of it, are you sure he did not learn it from another as well as from you?

Secrecy is recommended to a director under pain sometimes of mortal sin. Theologians so decide, concerning all revelations which relate to temptations, evil tendencies, and to all that could defame the person who confides in him.

Certainly if the director is wanting in discretion you are not obliged to reveal your conscience to him again, but beware that your judgment of him is not a grave sin in itself.

"In regard to the manifestation of conscience, or direction, whatever it may be, we should know," says P. Cotel, "that directors are obliged to strict secrecy concerning all the confidence one may give them, and that they cannot even communicate it to their superiors without the consent of the religious."

Superiors may, when there is no question of sacramental secrecy, profit by such communications, for our good, and our personal guidance, and even for the good of the community; but on the express condition that they do nothing of a nature to reveal to others what has been confided to them.

Moreover, as a religious confides in a superior as a father, not as a judge, the latter has no right in consequence of this confidence, to take severe measures against his subject, though he is permitted sometimes to gently reprove him, and even to correct him by imposing some salutary and fatherly penance. In a word, superior and subject, in their relations with each other, must be animated solely by a spirit of love and charity.

The one opens his heart to find succor, light, consolation; the other meets him with special affection and kindness to sustain, help, encourage, and enlighten him, but not to severely reprove or punish him; and the superior is far from esteeming a subject less, who thus opens his heart through a motive of virtue !*

---

*The manifestation of conscience which the director has received, obliges him to observe absolute secrecy, even concerning virtues and special favors from God. It is upon this principle, that P. Regnora, does not fully approve the conduct of some confessors who, after the death of their penitents, make known the singular privileges of innocence or virginity with which they were favored, when the confessors have no knowledge of these things, except through the confessional.
—Schram.

7th. **My Director says nothing to me, or always reproaches me.**

The first is a very trifling objection. Profit by the little he says to you, and you will become a Saint.

Are you not yourself to blame for his reserve, with your distrustful timid manner, your reluctant words, your half avowals, your vague declarations?

Go to him frankly, and he will be open with you. " Do not wish," wrote Mother Emilie, "that your superior should say a great deal to you.... If you are simple, like a child, a few words will be sufficient for you."

" We should beware," says Fr. Faber, " of driving our director into much speaking, either by acting on his human respect, or his natural kindness, or wearying him by importunity. There is, after all, little to be said where growth is so slow as it is in the spiritual life. A conversation between an oak and the woodman would surely come to an end soon, if growth and development, blight, birds, bees, and ivy, were the only subjects of conversation, and it was not allowed to pass into idle, irrelevant matters. For an oak does not make an inch a month, either of trunk or twig, and it could hardly expect to have its bark brushed, and varnished, and picked out with gold. So the soul is not revolutionized every day. To-day is yesterday's brother, and to-morrow's also.

"What is there to be said? All this talking leads to our making new starts in new directions, after each palaver. It is taking up devotions and throwing them down again, like a child restless amid his toys. It is heaping practices upon practices, and getting the fruit out of none of them. It is applying remedies, and then applying others before the first have had time to take effect. It is driving God."

Nor must you complain of the continual reproofs which you say you receive.

Either they are merited, and in this case amend, or at least show a good will to do better, and make some effort,—or they are not merited you believe, then humble yourself, be patient, offer to God the suffering the unfavorable judgment causes you, justify yourself with simplicity if you wish, but quietly and without any bitterness, and tranquilly await your justification, which will not be long in coming.

8th. *After seeking direction I return wearied and dissatisfied.*

Because you seek it only for consolation, when your sole object should be to find in it means of sanctification and of knowing the will of God.

Consolation is sometimes granted by God as a reward, as an encouragement, but it is not due.

It is rare, however, that God does not give it sooner or later; we promise it to you in His name, if you seek direction in a spirit of faith, with simplicity and an ardent desire to become better ; try.

This weariness and discontent, created by direction in which the heart has not been at ease, profoundly discourages the soul if she have not the strength to wait and generously accept the trial.

One of the causes of this discontent is our too eager desire to find in our director all the spiritual consolations we want, and if this desire is not satisfied, we are disconcerted, saddened, and we complain.

We believe that all interest on the part of the director has ceased, we doubt whether what he counsels is suitable for us, we want something different from what he tells us, and we consider ourselves desolate and abandoned.

Doubtless such souls do not seek direction from any reprehensible motive, but they would be relieved of a burden which oppresses them, find a support which will sensibly help them to rise above their miseries, that they may no longer feel the weight of the trials God sends them. In a word, they would like to feel themselves borne along the road to heaven, and avoid all fatigue and all difficulties. This is an opportunity for recalling the following words so fruitful in applications: "If it were thus, where would the martyrdom of life be?"

Generally the mission of a director is to teach us to endure our trials more meritoriously rather than to lighten them,—to enlighten the soul upon its true interests,—to lead it to God and gradually lead it to rest in God alone.

Want of faith is another cause of this dissatisfaction and this weariness after confession as well as direction. Hear these words which were addressed to a soul like yours:

1st. "You lack faith in the grace of state granted to every soul of good will, enabling it to worthily approach the sacrament of Penance;—this grace attached to one's state is threefold: The first enables you to reveal your soul to your director as God wishes it to be revealed. Mark you, as God wishes it to be revealed, and not as you wish.

The second grace enables you to thoroughly comprehend the advice, the counsels of your director. You always comprehend them sufficiently when you seriously wish to understand and profit by them.

The third consists precisely in that immediate succor granted you by God to enable you to do His will manifested through your director who is His minister to you.

Have you faith in this triple grace? Alas! your disquiet convinces me that your faith on this point is null.

You lack faith in the grace of state possessed by your confessor. He also has a triple grace—the grace to hear you, the grace to understand you, the grace to answer you.

Admire here a delightful mystery. God gives the priest a supernatural hearing and in the sacrament of penance a hearing which may be called sacramental.

You wish to represent something to him one way, always, doubtless, in good faith and with an intention to act uprightly,—he, enlightened by God, understands it in a totally different manner. Is he in error? No, certainly not! He understands as God wishes him to understand. He gives you a decision which you did not expect, and this decision is from God, it is the only one you need at the time, and the more firmly you hold to it the nearer you will be to the truth.

You lack faith in confession, in the efficacy of the Sacrament, and the virtue of absolution. The sublime words of absolution have been uttered over your soul, you wished to be sincere, you have taken the usual precautions, you are not conscious of any obstacle to the grace of pardon. The sublime words have produced their effect.

You must believe this. Then never say: " I know not how to make myself known." We always know how to do what we heartily wish.

Do not say: "I am not known." God knows you; you go to the priest as to God, therefore the priest knows you. Know moreover that it is easy for a priest, had he ever so little experience in the guidance of souls, to recognize those whom God sends to him. He has grace for this.

150 *Objections to the practice of Direction.*

9th. *I would prefer to seek my direction in writing.*

Two motives impel us to this resolution. The first, hardly an acceptable one, to avoid the confusion we experience in speaking ill of ourselves; the second, a reasonable one sometimes, to be more free.

We leave these permissions to directors, but we think that when direction can be sought in person, it is better. (*See the decisions of the following Chapter.*)

When one is at a distance from his director, we most certainly do not prohibit writing him, we even recommend religious who have left the mother house, in which their novitiate was made, to write to their superior-general, nor do we censure letters written to a priest who formerly directed us and whom Providence has removed from us, provided this correspondence be sanctioned by obedience. We should not have those pages so full of salutary counsels written by St. Francis de Sales, Bossuet, Fenelon, if the pious souls to whom they were addressed had not been able to correspond with these men of God; but, here particularly, we enjoin prudence and reserve.

Our spoken words vanish, but our written

words remain. Doubtless directors preserve no letter containing intimate revelations of the soul, but one of such letters may be forgotten, or go astray.

Here again we have no precise rules to give, do as your directors allow you.

10th. *I am afraid of importuning and troubling my Director.*

This is one of the most specious pretexts of the devil, and one which makes most impression on timid souls. First of all, your director knows very well that he is there to be importuned, as you in your human language express it, but which he, in divine language, calls gaining merits.

Have you ever heard a merchant complain of being disturbed every moment to sell and make bargains ?—Have you ever heard a physician complain of the number of his patients ?—Your director is paid by God for every disturbance.

Do not forget that the revelation you make to your director of the interior sentiments of your soul, is the greatest mark of esteem and confidence you could give him, and that this confidence necessarily disposes his soul to pity, compassion, and affection.

But he is sometimes surprised into showing

temper, you say. Are you very sure? And if true, may it not be a weakness due to physical weariness, to the fatigue of long interviews which preceded your arrival, to an extra amount of work, which is pressing upon him....moreover, he will endeavor to make you forget, by greater attention to you, this moment of weakness, of which he quickly repented.

Do not, of course, be importunate, but also, do not be too timid, and above all, do not judge unfavorably.

When seeking direction, say only what is necessary—express it frankly—show yourself submissive and grateful,—do not obstinately or haughtily contest; have the good faith to simply believe without any ulterior thought, that one is hurried, when he tells you he is; take the suggestion, to come back later, simply as it is said, and not as an indefinite postponement, or a mark that you are troublesome,—show that you appreciate the advice you receive. In a word let confidence be apparent in your countenance and words, and be sure that you will always meet with a visibly kind reception.

CHAPTER SEVENTH.

Matter of Direction.

Before entering into detail upon what forms matter of direction, we think it necessary to give the following counsels which we find in *Les Principes de la Vie Religieuse*, par le P. Cotel, and in *Le Gouvernement des Communautes Religieuses*, par P. Valuy.

I.

General principles on the matter of Direction.

The general doctrine of ascetic writers on the manifestation of conscience which religious owe their superiors cannot apply equally to all superiors of communities. Doubtless, any one who enters the difficult way of perfection, should not wish to walk therein alone and undirected. and it is to aid, enlighten, and preserve souls from illusions that God has not only given them rules to follow, but also superiors to consult.

Nevertheless, we conceive that there is a great distinction to be made on the point in question, between superiors who are priests and superiors who are not. The first have the knowledge and grace of the priesthood, both of which are wanting to the second. The first being capable of exercising, and in fact possessing, jurisdiction, a religious may confide the secrets of his conscience under the sacramental seal of confession, which is impossible with the second.

Hence it manifestly follows, that the account of conscience such as the masters of the spiritual life speak of, is completely due only to superiors who are priests, and that the others can have no right to it, if there be any right about it, save in a much more restricted degree which we shall call direction.

In support of this conclusion, P. Cotel cites a decree of the Congregation of Rites which we will give later, and which makes the manifestation of conscience a point of perfection doubtless, but leaves it optional and not of obligation.

In religious Orders of women, and even of men where the superior is not a priest, three things are reputed as not falling under the rule concerning the manifestation of conscience :

That which relates to sin.

That which requires a theological decision.

Temptations of a nature to make one blush or excite the passions.

These things come within the province of confession.

Nevertheless, a subject trusting to the discretion of his superior, may in certain cases, for his profit and consolation go further than the rule requires on this point.

There are confidences which may be permitted but cannot be exacted.*

"In saying," remarks P. Gautrelet "that the object of the manifestation of conscience was not to reveal the sins one may have committed, we did not claim that a subject was prohibited from opening his soul to his superior on this point; this may be even necessary sometimes to make one's self known, but it has its disadvantages; there are even faults of a certain nature which it is not expedient, ordinarily at least, to declare outside of confession.

"Therefore we cannot too strongly recommend discretion on this point to superiors of religious communities; we could cite in support of this recommendation, certain facts

---

* "We must endeavor as much as possible," wrote Mère Emilie, "to conceal nothing from the person who directs us, if we would be safely directed, except that which concerns the most delicate of all virtues, on which subject we must use reserve and only express ourselves according to our needs in the holy tribunal."

amusing in their absurdity, but for the painful feelings excited in our heart by the abuse of power in a thing so sacred, and the species of profanation which results therefrom, to one of the most august sacraments of the Church.

" Happily these aberrations are rare.

"If there was ever a founder of an Order who had the *practice of direction* at heart it was St. Ignatius : 'Let all,' he says, 'make themselves completely known to their superiors, concealing nothing from them; not 'even the depth of their own conscience.' Yet, what says Rodriguez, that man so versed in theology, and so perfect in the ways of God, in explaining this article of the constitutions of his holy founder? He teaches us that we must begin by distinguishing with great care that which is sin from that which is not,—and he declares on the one hand, that in virtue of this point of the rule, subjects should, in the manifestation of conscience, reveal to their superior all their imperfections, and infirmities, make known to him their failings, their evil inclinations, and tell him their faults ;—on the other hand, he states most positively that the intention of the rule and his holy founder concerning all that we call grievous sin, is

Matter of Direction. 157

that it be not declared out of confession. He even adds, that superiors should not question persons out of confession upon things which it is extremely shameful to acknowledge nor even permit them to speak to them of these things.

" ' It is in the sense of this decision,' adds P. Lafiteau, ' that we must understand the following paragraph in the constitutions of many religious Orders : *The novice, in taking the habit, should give her superior an abridged history of her life, of the good as well as the evil, reveal her temptations, her interior trials, discover her heart, and let its inmost recesses be known to her superior.* This does not mean that the novice is obliged to make a confession of the sins of her life to her superior. Thus the constitutions add that this manifestation should be made *summarily and briefly*, and be sufficient to enable the superior to better understand how to guide her."

The Congregation of Rites composed of Bishops and regulars established at Rome by the Sovereign Pontiffs, has several times said, in approving religious Institutes submitted to its examination :

" For the present, we restrict the manifestation of conscience to public transgressions of the rule and to progress in virtue, all the rest being treated of with the confessor; and this manifestation is also simply optional, not obligatory nor formally prescribed, and it must even be rendered verbally and not by letter."

A pious and learned ecclesiastic, consulted upon constitutions which were to be sent to Rome for approbation, thus expressed himself concerning manifestation of conscience :

"I think it indispensable to prescribe what follows in order to obviate a multitude of disadvantages and imprudences.

" 1st. That the sisters, though having to render with confidence and frankness an account of their interior dispositions to their superior, be in no way obliged to reveal to her their sins, past or present.

" 2d. That this account rendered, may in no way prevent the sisters from treating of their interior with perfect liberty and frankness with their confessor."

The theologian Collet states this case of conscience : "If a superior wishes to oblige one of her religious to reveal to her her most intimate thoughts, is the religious obliged to obey?" Here is Collet's reply :

"Certainly, confidence in the lights of a wise and experienced religious may be of much service to a religious. A superior who thoroughly knows his subject, sustains him when discouraged, moderates his excessive fears, reforms his vicious tendencies, confirms him in his good desires, secures him against the illusions into which timorous souls too often fall. It is upon this ground that the early solitaries wished that a religious should bear his heart in his hand when he went to his superior. But if we place this practice among the points of perfection and humility... it will be very dangerous to make it of precept, and more than imprudent to command anyone, whoever he may be, to reveal all that passes in his heart.

"Let us not forget that confidence springs from the heart and is not to be commanded. Above all, let us not forget that it has frequently been the ruin of those who gave it and of those who received it."

It was the grave abuses arising sometimes from exacting avowals in direction which led the Congregation of Rites to say, when approving in 1863 the constitutions of an Institute of Brothers: "All that is said concerning manifestation of conscience shall be effaced."*

Let us sum up these general rules by the following words of P. Gautrelet :

"The direction which the superior is to give is not usually a purely interior direction, but rather exterior, and in the interest of the order of the house; if she is to help the soul in the way of perfection, she should, particularly as superior, direct her subjects in the observance of the rule and discipline, and in the fulfilment of their duties.

" This remark is subject to modification when there is question of religious superiors who are usually priests ; we refer here only to superiors of Orders of women ; nor do we pretend to put upon the same level those who, in newly established congregations situated in the country have but two or three sisters with them.

---

* The decisions of the Congregation, whether general or relating to a special case, in no way weaken either the necessity for perfection or the advantages of direction.

They are but a guarantee of the perfect liberty allowed a soul to manifest her conscience out of the confessional.

They confirm by their authority this wise rule which religious superiors had already understood, that there can be neither exacted nor asked in direction, any avowal of past faults, or of faults likely to be committed again.

Finally, they enlighten and reassure timorous souls who, always fearing on the one hand that they have not made themselves sufficiently known, and on the other, not daring to speak of their faults, live in great anxiety.

Matter of Direction. 161

" The question of direction in their case is still more simple, and the account of conscience, if it should exist at all, is reduced to a very small matter."

II.
Subjects which may serve as matter of Direction.

A virtue to be acquired, or a fault to combat. Behold the matter which may be called the foundation of all direction, and which, though we have nothing special to say, will always furnish the director an opportunity to give a counsel, and the soul directed an occasion to speak of her efforts.

Your first care should be to ask your director : What is the virtue I must endeavor to acquire? What is the fault I must combat ?

Then, when you go to him, say simply : I come to render you an account of my efforts.

Then state the repugnance or attraction you feel in practising the virtue ;—repugnance or attraction : these two sentiments alternately predominate in each of us, without our being able to account for the cause which produces them ; be not alarmed then at the sudden change you will sometimes experience in your soul.

State your efforts, or the little courage you have had to overcome yourself.

The acts you have produced, or those which you have allowed to escape you through negligence, ill will, or lassitude...

If necessary, in the beginning, note in writing, your gains and your losses. That is tedious you say; yes, no doubt, but is not the perfection of your soul worth the trouble you would so readily take for the advancement of your fortune?

The virtue to be chosen first of all is fidelity to your rule and your exercises. This is where we must always begin, and it is not possible to advance in virtue without this *fidelity* which gradually breaks and subdues the will and prepares it in a most special manner to receive God's graces.

Answer the questions which are put to you,—accept with simplicity praise, encouragement or punishment.

Do not hesitate to recall the same thing each time you go to seek direction, if necessary; it is for your director to judge of your advancement and your efforts.

**

Here are other subjects which offer abundant matter:

1st. *Actions.*

If there has been any particular incident in our daily life, and the effect it has produced upon us,—some folly, some frivolity, some thoughtlessness,—some humiliation, some failing....and what have been, or what are, the consequences we dread.

If there has been any remarkable action : merited praise,—commendation received...

If there have been any acts of virtue performed before God alone.... Tell them all with simplicity ; it is not vanity, but a need to be known and encouraged ; do not be deterred by the thought that you are impelled by self love.... Leave your director to humble you, he will know how to find occasions of doing it, if God so inspire him; but always act with simplicity.

Speak of the good actions you have omitted through indolence, want of zeal, through human respect, those which you have performed through habit without the intention of offering them to God.

You will see how this attention to render an account of your conduct will accustom you to act for God and to fill your life with meritorious actions.

We must manifest with simplicity, say the

Instructions of the Visitation nuns, whatever inclination or facility for virtue we find in ourselves; reveal the lights we have received from God; the good principles we entertain, our projects for advancing in perfection; mark the sentiments and inclinations which the Holy Spirit produces in the soul; our relish for the things of God; the attraction which He gives for prayer and the interior life; whether we are inclined to the practice of humility, of obedience, of mortification, of all the other virtues and in what way.

2d. *Temptations.*

Speak to your director of the temptations you experience, even though you in no way consent to them, particularly of those which are most usual.

"We sometimes persuade ourselves," says Tronson, " that it is not necessary to speak of the attacks of the evil one because we repel them; nevertheless it is of the greatest importance for the director to know them, in a community particularly, because not knowing our temptations he may counsel us things which he may have reason to believe useful and which temptation would render dangerous to us."

Matter of Direction. 165

Then, should he not give us the means to resist ?

Some inexperienced souls imagining a multitude of temptations to be a mark of being abandoned by God, of weakness, of a want of generosity, ... blush to thus find themselves the sport of the evil one, and dare not, through fear of being despised, or thought guilty, make known their state.

These souls are in error. The greatest Saints were a prey to the most frightful temptations ; God permitted it, to render them more vigilant, to give them an opportunity to manifest greater fidelity, to keep them in humility, to render them particularly more compassionate for others.

Then tell your temptations with simplicity ; and your director, so far from experiencing a feeling of repulsion, will be filled with pity and compassion. State, if known to you, the origin, source, cause, of these temptations, tell particularly how you resist them.

Be prudent when there is question of temptations against the holy virtue ; speak of these only in general terms, if your director is not a priest, and reserve the avowal of your faults for confession.

There are five kinds of temptations of

which we should particularly render an account:

Temptations against the commands imposed upon us.

Against the counsels given us.

Against our vocation, and our state.

Against the charge confided to us.

Against any particular person, and even against our director, whom we suspect of not liking us.

"A holy religious," says Mgr. Rey, "informed me that the evil one, the first enemy of salvation, rejoices very much at one thing, viz.: that a religious should not like to seek direction and particularly to make known his temptations; for in this case, victory is assured to the evil one, he fights in single combat now, woe to him who is alone!

"There is nothing, on the contrary, which the devil dreads so much as being discovered; an evil-doer fears the light. And the devil, who is the spirit of darkness, finding himself and his snares revealed, loses hope of victory, and takes flight.

"The devil wounds in silence: a serpent is hidden beneath a stone; rash one, if you put your hand under it, you are bitten; but raise the stone, expose the serpent, and he will instantly take flight.

"Behold the conduct of the devil, who retires when he is exposed to the light ; as he is a monster of pride, he likes not to find his impotence and weakness discovered, and flies covered with shame. Then raise the stone, tell your director of this temptation and the serpent will hide himself in his caverns!

"Raise the stone, and tell your director this inclination for possessions, money, little articles of furniture, etc.

"Relate without constraint your temptations against sobriety in eating, your temptations to reserve bread, wine, meats and other things, and the evil one is vanquished."

3d. *Ennui.*

Hours of sadness, discouragement, sufferings of heart, sufferings of soul, their real or supposed cause, the resistance we made, the consolations we sought,—here are almost inexhaustible subjects.

In seeking direction, sometimes the hour is spent in tears. Let your tears flow, let them flow, poor afflicted soul, and do not fear to meet with cold, unsympathetic words which will close your heart. Where should you go to pour forth this burden which is killing you, if not to that heart friend who replaces the hearts you left in the world and to whom the Heart of Jesus has given His love?

"God tries us sometimes by withdrawing His sensible grace from us and leaving us to our poverty and darkness. He abandons us to certain fears and anxiety concerning our state, our past sins, our continual falls. Ceasing to make His voice heard, He wishes that we have recourse to those who hold His place, to learn how we should bear ourselves in the trials and difficulties which we encounter, such as contradictions, disappointments in the duties of life, which excite in us impatience, murmurs, complaints, vexations, repugnances. Frequently the ingenuousness of making known these sad and bitter impressions dissipates them and consoles us.

"Our frankness in using this remedy should go even as far as making known to the superior any trial we experience, or fear to experience through her. We should believe that her charity will enable her to rise above the pettiness of any personal feeling, and that she will be more concerned for the suffering she unwittingly causes you than for any personal consideration."

4th. *Inclinations and Dispositions.*

Towards certain faults : excessive talking, raillery, jealousy, for example— of such a person whom we like better than the others,—of such a charge, of such a study...

State particularly any opposition we feel for virtue.

This point is important, for the principal end of direction is to smooth the difficulties we find in the path of devotion where we have such great need of counsel, support, consolation and encouragement.

We find obstacles to virtue in our mind: doubts, perlexities, scruples, anxieties, which divert the attention from serious things and form an obstacle to prayer and the freedom necessary to perform our duties well.

We find obstacles to virtue in our heart and will, and these obstacles come from our weakness in resisting evil, and practising virtue,— from our levity, our inconstancy, from the alternate inclinations for good and evil which we continually experience,— from our insensibility to the things of God— from an inclination for all that flatters our pride and our self love,—from the joys and sorrows created in us by vain things,— from our too eager desires, our excessive activity, our caprices even in virtue,— our attachment to our own sentiments,— our discouragement and disrelish for virtue,— our aversion and our antipathy to our neighbor, and sometimes even to those upon whom we depend. . .

We cannot explain ourselves with too much simplicity upon these things, add the *Instructions Visitandines*, and particularly upon all that attaches the heart and turns the affections to creatures or anything which is not God,— or upon the evil habits we may have contracted, and the passions of which we are most frequently sensible.

Tell the projects for good with which God seems to have inspired you, speak without fear of the hopes you nourish, the ideas you voluntarily entertain.

Tell the virtue to which you are naturally inclined : is it devotion to others, activity in labor, a spirit of silence ? . . .

Dispositions of the body.

Sickness, indefinite indisposition, accidents, fatigue, the cause. . . . . Is it imprudence ? Is it your work ? We often fail in simplicity to make known our fatigue, and particularly, to accept the alleviation

Matter of Direction. 171

which it has been thought wise to suggest to us. We fear to appear, in the eyes of our superior, a character without energy, we keep up to the last, and thus we become useless through our own fault and even a burden to the community.

Dispositions of the Soul.

For holy communion, the manner in which we prepare for it, the recollection with which we make our thanksgiving, the decorum we observe on the day we have had the happiness of receiving Jesus Christ. * For meditation, how we make it, whether we follow the method, whether we like it, whether there is another which we prefer? For the different points of the rule, the intentions with which we observed them, the facility, relish or repugnance we experienced in observing them; — the thoughts which

---

* The confessor alone, has the right to regulate the number of our communions; and even in communities it is he who should give permission for the extra communions not prescribed by the rule.

Mgr. Landriot, in his beautiful work on Holy Communion, has added to the fifth conference a note on this subject which we think well to reproduce here:

" In a book printed lately and which contains moreover excellent things, do we not find certain exaggerations in a totally opposite sense to Jansenism?

"We read : ' The refusal of the permission to communicate more or less frequently, given by a spiritual director, is a counsel, and not a strict law binding the conscience. The

habitually occupy us ;— the graces with which God favors us ;—the books which lead us to God, those we read, and those we would like to read.

For devotions; what are those for which we feel most inclination? Are we easily moved before the Tabernacle, at the foot of the Blessed Virgin's altar? Does God cause us to experience joy and sweetness in His service, or are we cold, almost insensible, obliged to force our lips to tell God we love Him? Have we a special devotion to the Holy Eucharist, the Sacred Heart, the Blessed Virgin? What are our pious practices to honor Mary, to worthily prepare ourselves for Holy Communion? What are the pious thoughts which make most impression upon us?—Is it the fear of God's judgment, abandonment to divine Providence, confidence

---

right to communion, and even daily communion, is in fact a direct consequence of our baptism. We hold this right directly from Jesus Christ, and if we consult on this point an enlightened priest penetrated with the spirit of the Church, it is not that he may grant us this privilege, but help us to make a holy use of it.'

"Are not these words formally opposed to the decrees of Innocent XI. and to the decision of the Roman Congregations? According to these decrees it is the confessor who is to judge of the frequency of communions, and we must conform ourselves to his judgment.

"'To say that one need not follow the advice of his confessor for communion, is according to theologians, an opinion opposed to the common teaching of the Doctors and to the practice of the Church."

in our Lord, a tender and filial trust in Mary?

Dispositions of the mind.

The studies we prefer, our readings, the course of reading we would like to follow... The direction of the mind is a very vast field which may, according to circumstances, give occasion for very useful counsels.

What useful labors have been accomplished for communities owing to the impetus, encouragement and counsels afforded by direction!

How many religious, men and women, with but an imperfect knowledge of their ability and intelligence, would have spent their lives in puerile useless labors, had they not been guided by their superiors, to whom they simply submitted their writings and whom they obeyed as God Himself!

What treasures of intelligence buried through humility, indolence, or timidity, the word of a director has brought forth! And on the other hand, what errors of doctrine avoided! what illusions destroyed! what troubles prevented! Generally, distrust any project, any thought, any idea of perfection promising great results, when we hesitate to make it known to our superiors.

Daily Life.

Permissions to be asked and renewed,—points of the rule to be expounded and explained,—difficulties of every kind to be solved—an account rendered particularly of the manner in which we perform our labor and the forbearance we exercise towards those who labor with us.

We think it well to reproduce here the following pages from our *Little Manual of Novices* :

A novice, more than all others, needs direction. The religious life is new to her ; all that she sees, all that she hears, astonishes her, and makes her wish to be enlightened upon a multitude of details which she needs to know ; the questions which press into her soul form matter of direction. The novice easily experiences disquiet, disgust, weariness, from a multitude of causes ; at times there are even regrets in this poor heart which was so strong in the hour of sacrifice and believed that its strength could never be shaken ... Must there not be some outpouring of these trials, and these vexations? This outpouring is matter of direction.

The novice understands piety as it is frequently understood in the world: with self-chosen, sweet, easy, independent practices, free from any precise rule,— free particularly from sacrifices and contradictions; and she is grieved at not being able to pray as much as formerly, at finding herself restricted to a certain method of prayer which does not please her, at no longer feeling any relish for Holy Communion, and she becomes discouraged and alarmed... To calm this trouble, must she not expose the state of her soul? This exposition is matter of direction.

The novice hears readings and instructions which are all new to her; they speak of the maladies of the soul; of the means of recognizing them; of the remedies to be applied to them; of the obligation of a religious to become perfect, etc... Books give only generalities; must she not have that explained which she only partially understands? These explanations are matter of direction.

We see that direction is an outpouring of the heart,— the communication of intimate joys,— consolation in trial,— alleviation in crosses,— strength to support our misery,—the rule applied to our weaknesses and our needs. In a word, it is salvation

Matter of Direction

made easy, life calm, and actions meritorious.

* *
*

The directories of religious communities usually give a formula of direction or account of conscience, or manifestation of conscience, as it is called in some houses. It is well to follow this faithfully. Here is the formula which we find in *Les Petits Traités*, composed by the Blessed De La Salle :

Points upon which each Brother should examine himself to render an account of his conduct.

First Week.

1st. Whether he encounters or has encountered any hindrance, from what source, and since when.

2d. Whether he has not had some trials of mind, or temptations ; by what they were caused, how he bore himself in them, whether he have not given occasion to them in some way ; what their effect was ; whether they have disappeared.

3d. Into what faults he has fallen since

the last account of conscience ; whether he fell knowingly and deliberately ; whether he took means to correct himself and what these means were.

4th. Whether he has striven to advance in the way of perfection, or whether he has diminished his efforts, and in what he remarks this ; what are the virtues he has tried more particularly to acquire ; whether he has had any inspirations, and whether he was faithful to them.

5th. To what he feels most usually inclined ; whether he does not yield to his humor ; whether he does not follow his natural inclinations or his repugnances.

6th. Whether he practices mortification of the spirit and the senses ; whether he has practiced any extraordinary mortification, and whether he did it with permission.

7th. Whether he has faithfully and fervently performed the penances imposed upon him ; whether he was unfaithful to them, how many times, and for what reason ; what were those he neglected, and whether the omission caused disedification.

Second Week.

8th. How, and with what interior dispositions, he receives humiliations, rebuffs, and contempt.

9th. With what disposition he receives remarks upon his faults, and reprimands, whether he profits by the latter to amend his life.

10th. Whether he daily accuses himself of his faults with simplicity, as if before God ; whether he does not, on the contrary, do it through habit, and without any feeling of repentance.

11th. What affection he has for obedience, and whether he is disposed to obey all that is enjoined upon him ; what difficulty or repugnance he experiences in obeying.

12th. Whether he is faithful to do nothing without permission and of his own volition, not even the least things ; whether, on the contrary, he has failed in this respect, how often, and whether he has thus given pain.

13th. Whether he strictly observes silence at home and abroad ; whether he has spoken to some of the Brothers in particular, or to outsiders ; whether these conversations were held with permission, and what was the nature of them.

14th. Whether he strictly observes the

Matter of Direction.

other rules of the Institute ; whether he observes them fervently or slothfully ; what are those in which he has failed, and for what reasons ; whether he respects them all as much as he should, and whether there are not some to which he is indifferent, or for which perhaps he entertains even contempt.

15th. Whether he is faithful to be equally recollected at home and abroad ; whether he frequently, or rarely, enters into himself; whether he lives in habitual dissipation of spirit and the senses, whether he frequently recalls the presence of God ; whether he refers all his actions to Him, and performs them with the intention of pleasing Him.

Third Week.

16th. Whether he is assiduously faithful to all the exercises ; what are those in which he has failed ; how and with what intention has he acquitted himself of them.

17th. In what book he has made his spiritual reading ; whether, during this time, he has not read other books than those which were given him for this purpose ; whether he is in the habit of reflecting upon what he reads ; whether he applies it, and whether he derives fruit therefrom.

18th. What special fault has been the subject of his particular examen ; what means he has taken to correct it, and whether these means were efficacious.

19th. How he has made his meditation ; what fruit he has derived therefrom ; whether, during it, he has been particularly careful to keep himself in the presence of God, and in what way ; whether, he has followed the method proposed ; upon what subjects he most usually meditates ; whether, before concluding, he takes resolutions, what they are, and whether he is faithful to them ; whether he has a relish and facility for this holy exercise, or whether he experiences in it difficulties and dryness ; whether the difficulties he encounters and the repugnance he may feel for it do not render him less assiduous in practising it.

20th. Whether he has always gone to confession with the community ; whether he has any feeling against the Confessor ; what is the reason for any he may have ; whether he profits by his confessions.

21st. Whether he feels an attraction for Holy Communion, with what dispositions he approaches the Holy Table, whether with fervor and devotion, or with sloth and tepidity ;

Matter of Direction.

whether he voluntarily frequents it, what fruit he derives therefrom ; whether he dispenses himself from the Holy Table without permission.

22d. How he assists at mass, with what dispositions, with what attention ; whether he assists at the holy Sacrifice according to the method prescribed, or follows another method ; what is the other method !

Fourth Week.

23d. Whether his charity for his brothers extends equally to all ; whether his affection for them is not natural; whether he loves them only in God ; whether he has not had some feeling against some of them ; what was the cause of it, and whether it continued for any length of time.

24th. Whether there is not some Brother for whom he has a particular friendship, or with whom hes ha intimate intercourse, prohibited by the rule.

25th. Whether he likes his charge, and the exterior exercises of his profession ; whether he acquits himself of them punctually and faithfully and according to the rules, or whether he is indifferent to them.

26th. How he conducts the school ; whether he observes the rules ; what are those in which he most frequently fails ; whether he does not yield to impatience ; whether he neglects anything ; whether he does not lose his time, and how he employs it ; whether he has changed nothing in his class, introduced some innovation ; whether he was faithful to follow the lessons, to correct all faults, and for this purpose, made use of the signs prescribed in the *Conduite des Ecoles ;* whether he has not spoken to some of the scholars without necessity and too familiarly ; whether he has constantly observed a becoming reserve and circumspection in his intercourse with them ; whether his attentions and charity are equally bestowed upon all.

27th. Whether he earnestly endeavors to make his pupils advance in reading and writing ; whether of himself he has not changed the pupils' lessons, and for what reason ; whether order and silence reign in the school, if not, for what reason.

28th. Whether he is zealous for the instruction and the salvation of the children; whether he consequently devotes himself principally to inspiring them with piety ; whether he vigilantly watches over them during prayer, the holy sacrifice of the Mass, and the

Matter of Direction. 183

other religious exercises, to see that they bear themselves with proper modesty and respect ; whether he has taken pains to teach them the Catechism ; whether many or only a few of the children know it ; whether he teaches it to them every day ; whether he prepares himself for it as he should, and whether he teaches it in a way calculated to give them a knowledge of Christian Doctrine, by developing the Catechism text with questions and explanations suited to their capacity.

29th. What has been his treatment of the pupils ; whether he has not been too harsh, or too lenient ; in what spirit, with what feelings, and in what way he has corrected them; whether he has not done it through temper, impatience or even passion; what good or bad effects resulted from his corrections.

30th. Whether he has not dispensed himself from Holy Communion without the consent of the Brother Director, or even without the order of the confessor, or through a want of devotion, and without any legitimate reason, and how often this has happened.

* *
*

Here certainly is abundant matter of direction.

What soul then, after attentively reading this Chapter can still say: "I know not what to say when I go to seek direction," or, "I derive no profit from seeking direction?"

Then seek direction, guided by a spirit of faith, and convinced that you are going to speak to God's representative, to a soul whose special mission is to hear you, to understand you, to strengthen you, to counsel you, to sanctify you.

Seek direction with simplicity. Let your director read your heart as an open book, let there be no secret recess or corner hidden from him, no reticence or half avowals ; reserve for the confessional all that comes within the province of confession, but apart from your sins and, as we said, things of a nature to wound modesty, tell your fears, your projects, your desires, your vexations, your disappointments, your joys, your successes.

Peace, security, joy, are only purchased at this price.

Go for your direction at the time marked for it. God attaches a special grace to this submission of a soul which does not act by its needs alone, but by God's will.... But do **not** wait for the days marked, if you are haunted by temptation, disquieted by fear, oppressed by uncertainty, tormented by an indefinable trouble and weariness. Go without fear to your director and tell him simply that you need him, and be sure that you will return to your daily life calmed, strengthened, resigned and sometimes, even joyful.

CHAPTER EIGHTH.

Particular Counsels for Direction.

We shall speak in this Chapter of the character of pious persons,—of the different states in which they may find themselves,—of how they should comport themselves in these different states, and finally, we shall give, after St. Ignatius, a few rules for discerning whether what passes within us comes from God or the evil one. An extremely important matter which will help the soul to know herself, and particularly, to make herself known, and which will help her to appease her disquiet, when God permits that she is unable to see her director.

I.

Character of pious persons.

"Among those who seriously labor to acquire solid piety and attain perfection, there are some who are of a cold phlegmatic disposition, others are naturally sad and melancholy, others, finally, have an ardent sensitive nature. All these persons need to be differently directed, and all have different illusions to avoid.

1st. Those who are of a cold, phlegmatic disposition should beware of wishing to walk in the path of virtue with those who are of an ardent, sensitive nature. The former will struggle in vain to resemble the latter. God does not ask it. Each nature has its grace and its way of attaining sanctity. They should not grieve at not experiencing the fervent sentiments which they observe in sensitive souls, but console themselves with the thought that notwithstanding the dryness of their heart, notwithstanding the weariness they experience in all their spiritual exercises, they may yet greatly please our Lord, by a true desire of perfection, and an apostolic zeal for the glory of God and the salvation of souls. The generous accomplishment of duties, stripped of all spiritual sensibility renders them more pleasing to God, as it proves them possessed of more detachment from self, and more real devotion ; for it is neither a desire of consolation, nor personal satisfaction which impels them to be faithful, but only a principle of duty, and a sincere desire to please God. In the midst of the difficulties and trials arising from their disposition, they have need to remember frequently that true love of God is manifested rather by works than by affections and words. "If you love me, keep my commandments;" says Our Lord. " My little children, let us not love in word, nor in tongue," says the Apostle, " but in deed and in truth."

2d. Persons of a sad, melancholy, pensive, self-concentrated disposition are naturally inclined to consider the terrible truths of faith, to exaggerate the difficulties of virtue, and to magnify the faults they commit.

They are inclined to examine and scrutinize every recess and corner of their hearts, and to abandon themselves to discouragement.

Such persons are greatly to be pitied, they need firm, kind direction. They should apply themselves to the consideration of the consoling truths of our holy Religion, and absolutely prohibit themselves, as far as it is in their power, all reflection, all examination, which narrows the heart. Let them place with simplicity at the feet of Jesus Christ their spiritual infirmities, their faults, and their continual infidelities, and always rise with new courage. If, to use their own words, they find no means of advancing in virtue, let them try to advance in forgetful-

Particular Counsels for Direction. 189

ness of self and in confidence in God. This is what Our Lord earnestly asks of them.

For such persons, their safeguard against the troubles, anxieties and remorse of a timid, pusillanimous conscience, is faithful submission to a confessor. This submission is better for them than the most minutely detailed confession.

3d. An ardent and sensitive nature is capable of great things, but it is also exposed to great illusions and grave wanderings. Such a character naturally seeks devotion and sensible consolations. He wishes to advance but, with all his strength, rapidly, and after his own fashion. He is inclined to extraordinary things, to corporal penances, and all that nourishes and excites his sensibility. He feels keenly at one time the attractions of grace, the reproaches of conscience, his infidelities, his ingratitude ; at another, an excessive propensity to evil, and the most violent attacks of temptations of every kind. These alternate emotions of good and evil fill him with anxiety, and disturb him extremely. He seeks good too impetuously and repels evil too fiercely ; he is astonished to still find himself so far from perfection. He vainly sighs for that serenity of soul and silence of the passions which are the fruit of long tried virtue, or the effect of a happy temperament. Persons of an ardent, sensitive nature should be very distrustful of all that agitates them, of all that nourishes their sensibility, even in spiritual things. They should labor with sweetness and perseverance to gradually moderate their too great natural activity, to endure the instability of their heart, and to render their piety mature and *reasonable*, rather than sentimental and affecting.

II.

Different states of pious souls.

A state of consolation.—We call " Consolation, all that inclines the soul to the love of God, to detachment from creatures ; all increase of faith, hope, and charity ; peace, tranquillity, compunction of heart, docility and spiritual pliableness."

When the consolation is sensible, the soul is filled with ardor, she sighs for Our Lord, she bewails the little she does for His love ; she feels she is far from being all that He desires ! Deeply touched at all that God has done and daily continues to do for her, she would redouble her prayers, her pious practices, her penances. At times she is all on fire, so to speak, and nothing is difficult, nothing a burden, for grace upholds her.

Let the faithful soul observe great prudence and discretion in this state of spiritual abundance ; let her moderate all these ardors, and beware of giving herself too much to these sensible consolations.—She should only value them in proportion as they strengthen her will in good.—Let her humble herself and reflect how weak she will be when God abandons her a little to her own strength, for the time of trial will not be far distant.

Yes, the faithful soul should be very prudent in a state of sensible consolation, for it is particularly at such times, that the angel of darkness transforms himself into an angel of light, that he may ensnare her with illusions.—He excites her to excessive penances, long prayers, multiplied pious practices, and all for the purpose of overwhelming her, wearying her, making her attached to her spiritual practices and perform them through caprice.

2d. A state of desolation.—" Desolation is the opposite of consolation ; thus, all that leads the soul to base and terrestrial things, all weakening of faith, hope and charity, all trouble, anxiety, discouragement, dissipation, all attachment to one's own ideas, and intractableness, is desolation."

In this state, the soul no longer feels these heavenly ardors, these loving transports, these generous desires to labor and suffer for Jesus Christ. Spiritual things no longer move her; prayer is a burden to her; she is indifferent to Holy Communion; she would keep away from the Holy Table. She feels all her unworthiness, and what is more painful, cannot even bewail it. If she weeps, her tears seem to flow, not through love for God, but through pusillanimity, vexation, self-love. Perverse imaginings, thoughts more than worldly, sensual attractions have taken the place of her pious thoughts, her sentiments of compunction and repentance. Temptations against faith and hope have replaced the abundance of heavenly light and filial confidence in God. She can hardly be faithful to the most ordinary pious practices; this soul, which formerly could not find sufficient time to pray and converse with God. Finally, she believes that God repels her, because of her numerous infidelities and base ingratitude.

If the state of trial is not always so violent,

it is none the less crucifying. This kind of insensibility, or spiritual torpor is not rare in the ways of God, it is in itself a great cross to a naturally sensitive soul, which has formerly tasted how sweet God is. If her tears at least could flow, but this consolation is denied her. Her heart is in exile."*

III.
How pious persons should bear themselves.

To avoid falling into illusions in times of consolation, and yielding to discouragement in times of desolation and dryness, the only means is to freely open our heart to our director and completely submit to his decisions.

It is he, when we are not subject to a rule in a community, who should regulate the time to be given to prayer, the method of making it, sometimes even the words in which we address God.

It is he who should regulate our corporal penances, add, retrench, modify, as he thinks proper.

He who should choose our spiritual reading, and know all the books we read.

---
* P. Boone.

He who should be kept informed of our good works, of those we wish to abandon, the new ones we wish to undertake and the motives which actuate us.

To him should be confided our efforts, our progress in virtue, our spiritual joys, the trials God sends us.

It is he who should regulate our confessions, even to the manner of our accusations, if he judges proper; our communions, even the manner of preparing for them and our thanksgiving.

In a word, we must renounce our own views to follow those of the director. Despise, through obedience, the fears and troubles which would keep us from Holy Communion, simply make an act of contrition when the soul is disturbed by fear, and go forward at his word. This act of contrition and obedience takes the place of the most minute confession and consequently may calm any reasonable soul seriously desiring to love and serve God.

If this tranquillity, the fruit of obedience, is not sensible, it is reasonable and real; that is, there are real and well founded motives for being reasonably tranquil, though the tranquillity be not sensible. Sensibility is in no way required.

Particular Counsels for Direction. 195

Then let us be thoroughly convinced that any one who desires to advance in virtue, whatever his character, age or condition, has great need to *obey*. It is obedience which indicates and prescribes the means of perfection proper to every character, every age, every condition ; obedience, which wisely and prudently adapts these means to our degree of virtue or weakness ; obedience, which discriminately and gently modifies them according to circumstances. It is obedience which wards off dangers and illusions. She judges with a coolness and impartiality which we could not exercise in our own cause, If obedience exacts the greatest submission, the most complete, and oftentimes the most difficult abnegation, she also obtains very great graces and signal favors from God.

" The obedient man shall tell of victory. "

IV.

Rules for discerning the spirit of God.

We shall only indicate the principal ones after St. Ignatius, Cardinal Bona, Alvarez... These indications though briefly stated may be of great service to a soul who sincerely desires sanctification.

1st Rule.—*The spirit of God is recognized by its fruits.*

This is a fundamental rule, it rests upon the words of Jesus Christ. "By their fruits you shall know them.... the evil tree bringeth forth evil fruit." Let us observe, however, that there is not question here of certain good works in particular, but of the sum of one's good works.

There may be illusion in a particular work, but the illusion cannot affect the sum of a long series of good works.

Hence we must conclude : 1st. That a soul faithful to observe the law of God and the obligations of his state, who loves to practice charity, to perform corporal and spiritual works of mercy, who never deliberately omits one of his duties even the smallest.... is impelled by the spirit of God.

2d. That the soul who knows how to judge and speak of the excellence of virtue and perfection, but when occasion offers does not practice it, who knows in what patience consists, but complains and gets angry when another offends against him... is not completely filled with the spirit of God.

Let us remark, however, that we must regard as impelled by a good spirit one who is generally faithful notwithstanding occasional defections.

2d Rule.—*The spirit of God is recognized by the interior affection and intention to please and serve God.*

Hence we must conclude : 1st. That when exterior good works are accompanied with laudable interior sentiments, such as the intention to please God, to expiate one's sins, to win souls to God, etc., these works are the effect of the spirit of God.

2d. That a soul which frequently thinks of God, which habitually lives in the presence of God, and which is restrained by the thought of this presence, is impelled by the spirit of God.

A fervent spirit zealous for the good of its neighbor, though its fervor exceed sometimes the just limits of prudence, is good at least in substance.

3d Rule.—*The spirit of God is recognized by a deep humility.*

Hence we must conclude : 1st. That a soul which likes to speak of itself, which seeks to be seen, which delights to contemplate its works, is not impelled by a spirit of God.

2d. That a soul which endeavors to conceal some of its charitable actions, which controls and repels every disparaging thought of its neighbor, which unaffectedly seeks the society of an inferior, which stifles by a thought of faith every murmur which arises in its heart, is impelled by a spirit of God.

4th Rule.—The spirit of God is recognized by a calm and resigned acceptance of the mortifications which God sends.

Hence we must conclude : 1st. That it is not the number of mortifications one imposes on himself which indicates the spirit of God, but the generous accepting of those mortifications which God sends. To endure contempt without manifesting resentment, correction without seeking to justify one's self, to live for a time under an unfavorable judgment, and to neglect no duty, manifest indeed the spirit of God.

2d. That the soul inclined to mortify herself by cutting off certain enjoyments, by retrenching superfluities, by denying her senses, if she does all she can to conceal from every one her privations, her sufferings, her self-denials, if particularly her only object be to render herself more pleasing to God by overcoming her senses which divert her thoughts from Him or to expiate her sins...is impelled by the spirit of God.

5th Rule.—*The spirit of God is recognized by docility of mind.*

Hence we must conclude: 1st. That a soul manifesting a simple, affectionate, complete obedience to her superiors, and to her directors, with the ever-present thought that God makes known to them what He requires of her, is impelled by the spirit of God.

2d. That a soul who, even in the acquisition of virtues, and the pursuit of perfection, goes neither more rapidly nor more slowly than she is commanded, even though she may not recognize the wisdom of the command, who conforms herself in *all things* with fidelity and humility to the will of her spiritual guide, is certainly impelled by the spirit of God.

CHAPTER NINTH.

Direction in practice.

We can better compass the end of this Chapter by giving a practical illustration of direction, that is a pious conversation, between a soul and her director. We shall see, by the following dialogue, with what simplicity we must expose the state of our soul, the manner of making this exposition, the questions we may ask,—the objections we may offer,—the submission finally with which we must receive the decisions and counsels given us.

These pages are taken from *L'Esprit de la Mère Emilie*, an excellent work, in which pious souls will find counsels of great wisdom, and examples which will lead them to love virtue.*

---

* Mother Emilie, Founder and first Superior-General of the Congregation of the Holy Family in the diocese of Rodez, died in 1853. A decree signed the 27th of March, 1872, introduces the cause of her beatification and canonization. Her life is written by Leon Aubineau, and "*Her Spirit*," from which we borrow these pages, was written by Abbé Barthe.

First Direction.

Upon Humility.

The Superior:—Give me an account, my child, of your efforts against your predominant fault. Have you made your particular examen upon it every day?

The Religious:—Yes, Mother, I even keep a strict account of how many times I speak of myself during the day; but I confess I am not faithful to impose a penance on myself every time as you recommended. I really despair of ever becoming humble, for the more I apply myself to acts of humility, the stronger I feel my pride; when it does not manifest itself in actions, it does in thoughts which I would not dare to tell any one.

The Superior:—Do not be astonished at that; when we seriously devote ourselves to the acquisition of a virtue, we are usually strongly tempted to the contrary vice; and frequently the more we practice it the more empire the contrary vice seems to have over us because of the temptations which harass and trouble us.

But this empire really diminishes without our knowledge, so to speak, when we continue to struggle against the assaults which importune and weary us. Do not be discouraged, Sister ; only do not fail to inflict a slight penance upon yourself after each fault, such as making a very sincere act of contrition, devoutly kissing your crucifix, making a pious visit to some of the altars in the house, or kissing the floor three or four times with a feeling of contempt for yourself; and I beg of you do not let me hear you say again : *I despair.* We must despair of nothing when we have God's assistance, and you have it, Sister. He gives you light to know your faults, he gives you a desire to become humble, is not this already a great deal ? And have you not always had the grace of prayer which will obtain for you still greater succor ?... Oh ! my child, I have a strong hope that your desire will be granted, but not without humiliations. Come, tell me your thoughts of pride.

The Religious:—Mother, I dare not, besides I do not dwell upon everything that passes through my mind, and I even try not to remember it.

The Superior:—May it not be the fear of having to reveal these thoughts which makes you quickly reject them ? In that case you are influenced by a subtle snare of self-love. What do you think? Is not this your motive?

The Religious:—Yes, Mother, it influences me a little, but then, what necessity is there to reveal all that one thinks, when you do not consent to these thoughts and they give you pain?

The Superior:—If we would triumph over our pride we must humble ourselves; and one of the greatest acts of humility we can make is to simply reveal our miseries to the person who directs us. Certainly you are not obliged to tell all your thoughts of pride, but I think that God asks this of you, and if you refuse, you may be sure you will not be satisfied. Come, my child, pluck this thorn from your heart, tell me all.*

The Religious:—Mother, I dare not; let me wait until another time, it will cover me with confusion now.

The Superior :—How skilful the evil one is in deceiving us! Another time you will

---

*To act with this holy familiarity and thus simply question intimate thoughts, requires a childlike confidence between the director and the soul directed, which is the effect of grace, and supposes much virtue on the part of both.

No, a soul is not obliged to discover her intimate thoughts, but when she can do it, Oh! what happiness! what peace! what a guarantee of sanctity and of reaching heaven she ensures herself!

only find it more difficult; if you wait, he will keep you more and more occupied with your repugnance, and will even increase it, whereas, if you tell me all now, that will be the end of it. Come, Sister, courage, I am looking at my crucifix.

The Religious:—Well, I will tell you: I thought that if I wished, I could become one of the most learned religious in the Congregation; that perhaps, you would give me the office of Sister N.—, which would bring me in contact with Madame N.— and N.— and I should feel flattered. After my pupils' examination, I took much pleasure in the compliments I received, they recurred to me several times a day, and I longed for another examination. The fact that in the Novitiate I passed from the last to the first place in Instruction, made me think I had more ability than the others. I liked to remember also, that the Father in speaking of me to the Mistress of Novices, told her that I would make a good Mistress, and recommended me to her care. I like also to find myself with certain persons, even inferiors who tell me agreeable things. There, I am sure this is quite sufficient, Mother, you can understand all the rest.

The Superior:—If, instead of becoming

one of the most learned religious, you were to become one of the most fervent, would you not be satisfied? Well, that is what I want you to be. From the summit of pride, you must descend to the holy depths of humility. You are young, and believe me, when I tell you, you must wage serious war against a vice which may be your ruin, if you do not control it. I repeat, from the summit of pride, endeavor with all your strength and by every means to descend to the holy depths of humility.

The Religious :—I do not understand what you mean by the summit of pride and the holy depths of humility.... Do not, I beg of you, propose too great humility to me ; if I could not do all that you counselled me, I should have remorse for it all the rest of my life. I am always afraid that the thought of imitating you will enter my head, and I confess, I would not wish to do it.

The Superior :—" Do not propose to me, too great humility " ! do you understand what leads you to make such a request ? Ah ! it is perverse nature, grace does not speak thus ; on the contrary, it would impel you to beg me to counsel you the surest and shortest way to attain great humility, the essential foundation of all other virtues ; and at the cost of any sacrifice. It is of the last importance for you to combat your predominant fault, and to combat it tirelessly and unrelentingly. It is a general of an army with many soldiers under his command, who effects great ravages in souls; you must pursue it to the last, without being in any way alarmed, either by the violence, or the duration of the combat. God, the witness of your efforts, who in these combats, anticipates the soul, and sustains it by His grace, usually gives victory if you earnestly ask it. It is for love of Him, for His glory, that you combat, and fear not that He will fail to help you.

The Religious :—What then must I do?

The Superior :—Always the opposite of what pride suggests.

The Religious :—Shall I have the strength to do it?

The Superior :—God will give it to you. Thus, if you have committed a fault which will draw some censure upon you, do nothing to prevent it; if you are thought ill of, do nothing to change the opinion in which you are held; if pride leads you to do things which may win you praise, leave them undone, unless duty or obedience demands them; then purify your intention; if you want to be counted as something by your superiors, your companions, or even by persons outside, seek "to be unknown and esteemed as nothing,"* choose the last place everywhere and in everything, but unaffectedly.

The Religious :—Oh! that is so difficult! to avoid no blame, to permit one's self to be unfavorably judged when one word could destroy this false opinion, and reinstate you in the minds of others, no, I do not think I have the strength to do it always. But here is what I already thought of : I know my pride is great, and I am going to ask God to keep me always in humiliations, to permit me to be proud of nothing. I will say to Him : " My God, feed me with the bread of humiliations, steep me in the water of tears, wean me from my love for the esteem and favor of creatures ; make me an object of contempt ; may all that I do to exalt myself, turn to my confusion, so that I may be ever in abasement by the continual remembrance of my sins, by a profound sense of my misery." And as I am so fond of enjoyment, I would add : "Do not permit me to find satisfaction in aught here below, save in loving and pleasing Thee! Make eating,

---
*Imitation, B. 1, Chap. 2.

drinking and other natural satisfactions a cross to me ! I ask of Thee but one thing O my God : not to permit me to be lost eternally !"

This, dear Mother, is all I can do. I have already begun to address this prayer to God ; sometimes I tremble as I utter it, at the thought of great humiliations coming upon me, but I reflect at once that all these sufferings will be of little moment, if I have the happiness to be saved. Oh ! pray, pray for me, I beseech you.

The Superior :—I will, and I hope that you will become very humble. But at least do not let a day pass without asking God to give you this virtue of humility, which renders a soul so happy, which drew the Son of God to this earth. One day, the price of abjection will be clear to us. Believe me, my child, it is good to rest in contempt, to be counted as naught. Since you are very earnest in your desire to become humble, I am going to call your attention to certain things you did, in which there was more or less pride. When Sister N. told you, in my presence, that your pupils were too slow, that they lost time through want of being stimulated by the Mistress, you answered impatiently : " Ah ! what a trial those children are to a person of any spirit!" You should have contented yourself with quietly answering : "I will see that they do better for the future ; if I were more devoted myself, doubtless they would make more progress." When Mdlle N. was unable to answer what I asked her, you said very quickly : "I have told her that five or six times." If you had kept silence, you would have made a good act of humility. Yesterday morning, when I visited your class to assure myself that everything was in order, you hurried up stairs to see for yourself whether everything was in its place ; you should have let me pass first. When I said to you the other day, that the soup you made for the poor was not well made, you answered : "At home we do not make these soups." You should have said : "That is true, Mother, will you be kind enough to teach me how to make it?" See, my dear Sister, how we can profit by little occasions, to overcome our pride and practice humility, do not let such opportunities escape you as you have done heretofore.

The Religious :—Mother, you said a while ago that the vice of pride would be my ruin if I did not control it. Will you explain to me, please, how it might cause the loss of a soul?

The Superior :—It may cause its loss in several ways. A proud person is generally rash ; he fearlessly exposes himself to danger ; and if he perishes therein as the Holy Spirit threatens, we may say that pride is the cause of his being lost. A proud person is nearly always too tenacious of his own ideas, his own judgment ; he believes he has light superior to that of others ; and if he falls into error, there is no means, or at least it is very difficult to bring him back to truth. All the arch-heretics mentioned in ecclesiastical history were such, only because they were proud, obstinate minds. Any one may be deceived, but if he is humble he will be easily persuaded of his error, and above all will submit his judgment to the Holy Church, which is infallible ; but if he is proud, he will obstinately persist in his opinion and will "obey not the truth."—Rom. ii. 8. We probably will not become arch-heretics here ; but there are many errors which enter the mind of a religious, most dangerous errors which only humility can cure. Thus a religious may take it into her head that she would do more good if she were to go back to the world ; her superior, her confessor, who sees clearly that she runs the risk of being lost by renouncing her profession, tells her that she is about to commit an act of folly, of which she will repent too late ; they leave nothing undone to persuade her to remain ; if she is humble she will be convinced of her error ; if she is not, she falls into the snare the devil lays for her, and her loss is imminent, and it is pride which leads her to perdition. Another, still young, and with some talents, seeks very much to display them ; she yearns for praise. She is counselled to be as retiring as her functions will permit ; to fly praise, particularly from persons of the other sex, of whatever age or condition. But no, she must let every one see her trifling success in her class ; if she is not cloistered she tries to obtain a visit from the pastor, the curate, or some other person competent to judge of her supposed merit, and the progress of her pupils. If she had been humble and docile she would not have fallen into this disorder. Here is another who does not observe the Rule well; her confessor, her superior warn her ; show her that she is falling into a dangerous way ; they suggest some penances proper to correct her ; she omits these penances, or only performs them to be rid of them ; finding that her confessor and superior restrain her too much, she leaves her confessor to find one less severe ; she neglects to make her dispositions known to her superior, or does so very superficially. This religious who disregards the wise warnings of her confessor and of her superior will end by becoming blinded, and by falling into deplorable laxness ; and will owe her ruin to pride.

God detests pride in all His creatures, Sister, but particularly in His Spouses, He cannot endure it. Thus the shameful sins into which He sometimes permits souls consecrated to Him to fall, are a punishment of that vice which He pursues wherever it may be found, and still more in the souls whom He has honored so much as to make His own. Leaving the holy state of religion is frequently a punishment of pride and in my opinion the greatest.

The Religious :—Oh ! beg God, Mother, never to send me such chastisements ; I would a thousand times rather die than leave the Institute or fall into any grave sin. What you have told me has filled me with fear.

Direction in practice.

Second Direction.

Counsels on Piety.

The Religious :—I am glad that I am nearing the time for the annual retreat; I am going to ask permission to make a general confession of my whole life.

The Superior :—To rejoice at the approach of the retreat, and to prepare ourselves for it puts us in an excellent disposition for profiting by this great grace; but a desire to make a general confession may be a ruse of the evil one to make you lose time, and, perhaps, fill you with trouble; you must speak with the confessor about it.

The Religious :—But, Mother, this confession seems to me necessary; not to repair my past confessions, but to rouse myself from this state of tepidity into which I have fallen.

The Superior :—Who told you that you were in a state of tepidity?

The Religious :—No one, but I feel it.

The Superior :—It is for your confessor and your superior to decide the state you are in. No, my child, I for my part do not see that you are in that state of tepidity which would lead the good Master to reject you from His mouth.

The Religious :—Why is it, then, that I do not love God as I formerly did? I can hardly speak to Him any more in meditation; I find my prayers irksome and filled with distractions; I am ill at ease interiorly; I would rouse myself from this state.

The Superior :—This is simply because the good God wills for our advantage that we should not always continue in the same interior state. Love for God is not proved by feelings, but by works. It is not necessary to feel a relish for prayer and be free from distractions, it is sufficient to make it as well as one can; we have even more merit in praying without any relish for prayer and in the midst of unwilling distractions which we do our best to banish than with facility and sweet fervor. It does not satisfy our self-love, however, and hence our repugnance; but it benefits, purifies and strengthens our soul.

The Religious :—I would be consoled if I were sure that I did all I could to pray well; but how can I be sure?

The Superior :—One should ask her confessor or her superior, tell him what she does, and rest tranquilly upon his word. There is great merit before God in keeping one's self at peace through a spirit of faith, on the word of those charged to direct us.

The Religious:—Let me tell you, my dear Mother, the present state of my soul, and then I will follow your counsels, for my whole desire is not to displease God.

The Superior:—Certainly; but tell me, do you voluntarily dwell upon these distractions which assail you?—Do you neglect or cease to pray because you have no relish for prayer?

The Religious:—I think not. But I find it very trying during meditation and my visit to the Blessed Sacrament to be like a statue before God, or to have my mind filled with anything but the thoughts which should occupy me at that time.

The Superior:—Is it bad to be a statue, when it pleases God? Is it not a great honor? In the palaces of Kings there are statues which do nothing of themselves; but their presence is useful, they honor the master of the house. Why would you not honor God in this way if He wills it?

The Religious:—But when one's mind is filled with useless, even extravagant thoughts, how can you honor God?

The Superior:—By being very patient with one's self, saying to God in the words of a Saint: "Behold the fruit of my garden; that is all that is mine."

It is well to repeat a few lines of a pious canticle, or some verses of a psalm, forcing one's self to will what the words express. If we are incapable of doing it, then accept this state of impotence.

The Religious:—Would it not be better to read a pious book or say the Rosary?

The Superior:—In extremity one may do it, but we should only rarely have recourse to this means, for meditation is not vocal prayer or spiritual reading. One should do it, for example, when harassed by evil thoughts, for then the mind will be more easily diverted.

Third Direction.

Laxness.

The Superior:—Formerly it was you, my child, who feared, and I reassured you. But to-day you are without fear, and for that reason I fear, yes, I fear very much for you.

The Religious:—Mother, what do you mean? Your words and manner frighten me.

The Superior:—You do not understand me?... There was a time when you always feared to be estranged from God; you punished yourself, or asked punishment, for the slightest faults ; you came frequently to consult me; you did nothing without my assent; the fear of becoming tepid maintained you in fervor. But how is it with you now? Where have fled all those timid apprehensions which I liked to see, for they proved that you were not far from the good God.

The Religious :—True, Mother, I do not fear as I formerly did, yet I do not believe I do anything wrong,

The Superior :—I do not say that you do anything wrong, but there are things which, I am sorry to say, you have ceased to fear. What is that book which you have in your hand?

The Religious :—It is an abridged history of France ; I think it is approved, for Sister N— reads it.

The Superior :—A year ago you would not have read a book merely on the supposition that it was approved, you would have come and asked my approbation. You will tell me : this is not a bad book, others read it. That is not a sufficient reason for you to read it without my knowledge.*

Fear, Sister, fear, I repeat, to read profane books even when approved ; and as to pious

---

*Constitutions of the Sisters of the Holy Family, Explanations, No. 203, No. 273.

books bearing even episcopal sanction, ask before reading them ; for all may not equally suit you.

Come nearer, Sister, take off your belt, do you not see that your dress is too tight? You like a small waist ; is that fitting for a religious? The folds of your dress are arranged with too much care ; your veil is too low over your eyes, it was not modesty which prompted you to lower it in that way. Again, I tell you to fear, fear the approach of vanity ; I have just surprised you in one of its snares : it will lead you still further, you will, become, perhaps, its slave and victim.

Only a short time since, it was your delight to keep God's house, the sanctuary, in the most perfect order and neatness ; you never could give too much time to it ; and now, you hastily sweep the sanctuary, and use all possible haste in putting it in order that you may go to study, or other things which flatter your self-love. Fear, Sister, if you persist in thus withdrawing from God, God will end by abandoning you and, perhaps, irrevocably.

Formerly, you spoke but of God at your recreation, everything else wearied you. Is it the same to day? Now, you follow Nature which leads you to go with those Sisters whose humor suits your disposition, you seek to be well with everybody, you accept little flatteries ; here are imperfections which will lead you very far if you do not beware of them. Fear, Sister, fear to gradually replace the love of God which formerly reigned in your heart by a love of creatures. You will be unfortunate, believe me, if you withdraw from Him who formerly has been, and who alone can be, your happiness. What has become of that delicacy of conscience which made you fear the least evil, the slightest disobedience, the most trifling evasion? A slight criticism, or blame, a slight irreverence in choir, would be a subject of tears to you ; you frequently came to me, not daring to receive Holy Communion for reasons which appeared to me sufficiently slight ; and now you no longer come, yet I find you less faithful than you were then, much more reprehensible in certain things. Fear then, Sister, fear tepidity. Ah ! it is a dangerous evil to souls ! Tepidity has led many to perdition ; disregarding negligence and slight faults, its forerunners, they gradually fell into mortal sin ; and mortal sin at length precipitated them into hell.

The Religious:—Mother, I feel myself guilty, very guilty; I have been deluded, I see it now; pray for me that I may return to what I formerly was, and that I may not have the misfortune to be lost in the midst of the abundant succor with which this holy house abounds.

The Superior:—I will, most heartily, you may be sure. Return to me in two or three days; but pray, pray yourself a great deal, and do not be discouraged.

CONCLUSION.

As a summary and conclusion of our labor, we have gathered from the works of St. Liguori the doctrine of this Doctor of the Church on direction.

We know that St. Liguori, who to knowledge and sanctity adds great experience of souls, does not limit himself in his writings to speculations, but gives always numerous practical details which powerfully aid one in the conduct of life.

It was to present these details in full that we preferred not incorporating them in our work; it seemed to us that gathered together here they might be more profitable to religious, to whom they are principally addressed.

We are happy to be guided in practice by a doctrine in which the Church has found nothing reprehensible and which she proposes to all the faithful as a safe rule; and to accept the decisions which the holy Bishop gave only after he had implored on his knees the light of the Holy Spirit and the assistance of Mary.

I.

General Necessity of Direction.

"There are religious who pretend to live without a director; they think that, having rules and a superior, they need no other guide; but they are mistaken; for besides the rules and the superior, it is fitting that religious have also a director, that they may be counselled and guided in interior and even exterior exercises. 'It is true,' says St. Gregory, 'that some Saints have had God Himself as their immediate guide, but one should not wish,' he adds, ' to follow these examples, for fear that by disdaining the guidance of a man, we lead ourselves into error.'

"If a religious finds no director who can guide her in the way of perfection, God will supply her need; * but to refuse one of His ministers when we can obtain him

---

*Permit us to add here a few words of consolation for persons in the country, reduced to one priest, absorbed by the numerous exterior duties of the ministry, and who, unable to choose a director, do not find what seems necessary for the needs of their soul.

Jesus Christ is the first, or rather, the only director of souls. Address yourself to Him in all confidence; serve Him faithfully; come to your confession every week with a great spirit of faith, a sincere regret for your faults, a serious will to lead a regular and devout life, and be at peace; Jesus Christ with-

Conclusion. 223

is temerity which God punishes by permitting us to fall into many errors. God could direct us Himself, but to render us humble, He wishes that we submit to His ministers and that we depend upon their authority."

II.

Particular necessity of direction for scrupulous souls.

"The masters of the spiritual life indicate several remedies against scruples ; but all theologians, as well as ascetic authors, agree in concluding that the principal or rather the sole efficacious remedy is for the penitent to

---

out your knowledge will take upon Himself to teach you the secrets of the interior life ; it was thus He directed Mary of Egypt in the desert, and in infidel countries He directs Christians who scarcely see the missionaries once a year.

But neglect no succor within your reach ; read each day some solid, pious book ! " The Holy Gospels," " Introduction to a Devout Life," " The Imitation of Christ," "Short Lives of the Saints," "Spiritual Combat," " Visits to the Blessed Sacrament," by St. Liguori, and a small book of daily meditations may in a great measure suffice you.

If you are a female and can communicate in the parish with some truly pious person, that is attached to her duty, charitable in her words, submissive to the will of God, see her sometimes, though she may be unlearned in human things.

If an occasion offers of consulting a strange priest who comes for a *mission*, or a *retreat*, do it simply, without ostentation, but do not be deterred by human respect.

Do not complain of what is lacking you, and wait. God never fails any one, and He who feeds the birds of the air, will know how to afford your soul the food it requires.

wholly mistrust his own judgment and, placing himself in the hands of his spiritual father, blindly obey him. St. Philip Neri says that there is nothing more dangerous in affairs of conscience than to wish to guide one's self after one's own views. A scrupulous person who does not obey his director is lost. Not to yield to the decision of a director shows pride and a want of faith, says St. John of the Cross. In fact, Jesus Christ has declared that he who obeys His priests, obeys Him, and that he who despises them despises Him. *Qui vos audit, me audit; et qui vos spernit me spernit.*—Luke x. 16.

"Hence St. John of the Cross speaks thus in the name of the Lord: 'When you are wanting in docility to your confessors you disobey Me, for I have said: "He who despiseth you despiseth Me." He, on the contrary, who obeys his spiritual father cannot be deceived.' According to St. Bernard, what man commands, when he holds the place of God, provided it be nothing certainly displeasing to God, should be taken as a direct command from God Himself: *Quidquid vice Dei præcipit homo, quod non sit tamen certum displicere Deo, haud secus omnino accipiendum est, quam si præcipiat Deus.*—De Praec. and Disp.

"Thus the blessed Henry Suso assures us that God will not hold us accountable for what we shall have done through obedience. And St. Philip Neri taught the same to his penitents : 'Those who desire to make progress in the ways of God should submit to an enlightened confessor and obey him as God Himself; while we act thus we are sure of not being held accountable to God for what we do.' He added that we must have faith in our confessor, for God would not let him be deceived. For my part, I say that if a person becomes blind, his only resource is to take a faithful guide to lead him in the way he should go ; in like manner, a soul who finds herself in the darkness and confusion of scruples should allow herself to be directed by the guide God has given her and obey him blindly.—I say, by the guide God has given her, for, generally speaking, it is not well for a scrupulous person to speak of her doubts to other spiritual fathers than her own director, even if they should be holy and learned ; another, not knowing the state of her conscience, may ask her a question, or say a word to her not in accordance with the views of her own director ; and for this word, her conscience is again completely disturbed, and, losing the confidence she hitherto reposed in her own guide, she will remain forever, or at least for a long time, in disquiet and trouble.

"Then obey your director, my dear Sister, and be sure that in obeying him you cannot go astray.

"Thus did the Saints, who were likewise frequently tormented by scruples and fears of offending God, and by this means they ensured their safety. St. Catherine of Bologna was afflicted with scruples, but she obeyed her confessor in all things; if sometimes she feared to approach the Holy Table, a sign from her spiritual father sufficed to make her conquer her fears and go forward immediately and receive Holy Communion, therefore Jesus Christ appeared to her one day, and to encourage her still more to obey, told her to rejoice, for her obedience was very pleasing to Him. This good Master appeared also one day to Blessed Stephanie Soncino, a Dominicaness, and caused her to hear these words: 'Since thou hast remitted thy will into the hands of thy confessor, who is My representative, whatever grace thou wilt ask Me shall be granted thee.' She replied: 'Lord, I desire only Thee.'

"St. Augustine gave the same counsel to his friend, St. Paulin, who exposed his doubts to him, 'Go' he said, 'and consult some good spiritual physician upon your doubts and let me know what the Lord will have said to you by his mouth.'—We see that the holy Doctor held it as certain that if St. Paulin asked the advice of a spiritual father, God would speak to him and make known His will through His minister. St. Antony relates that a Dominican being very much tormented by scruples, another religious, who was dead, appeared to him and said : *Consule discretos et acquiesce illis :* Take counsel of the wise and hold to what they tell you.—The same Saint also relates that a disciple of St. Bernard was reduced to such a state by scruples that he was unable to say mass; but in his perplexity he happily went to consult his master, St. Bernard, who, without reasoning with him, contented himself with saying : 'Go, say mass, and let it be on my conscience.' The religious obeyed, and was forever delivered from all his scruples.

" We must not say: If I had St. Bernard for confessor I would obey as blindly, but my confessor is not St. Bernard.

"Doubtless, he is not St. Bernard; but he is more than St. Bernard, since He holds God's place to you. Hear the learned Gerson's reply to this : ' You who speak thus are in error; for you have not placed your confidence in a man because he is enlightened or holy, but because He is charged by God with the guidance of your soul, obey him then as God, and you cannot fail to do well.'—St. Ignatius Loyola at the beginning of his conversion was so beset by darkness and scruples that he could find no rest; but as he had real faith in God's words: *Qui vos audit, me audit,* he said with great confidence: 'Lord, show me the path I must follow : though Thou sendest me a dog for a guide, I promise to faithfully follow him.' He was in fact faithfully obedient to his directors; which availed him not only deliverance from his scruples, but also made him an excellent master for others. St. Teresa then had reason to say : 'Let the soul take her confessor as judge and give herself completely to his guidance, firmly resolved not to plead or think of her cause, confidently trusting in the words of our Lord : *He that heareth you, heareth Me.* This submission is very pleasing to God and powerfully helps us to conquer in the thousand interior combats we sometimes have to sustain, even though the judgment given upon our cause appear to us unreasonable, or we experience great repugnance in executing it. In a word, we accomplish the will of God!'

"If, then, Sister, when Jesus Christ comes to judge you, He ask you an account of what you will have done in obedience to your director, prepare yourself to make this reply : 'Lord ! I did that to obey Thy minister, as Thou didst command me to do.'—If you can then answer thus, you have no reason to fear that He may condemn you. Fr. James Alvarez assures us that, even though the confessor be mistaken, the penitent in obeying him cannot err, and walks in safety. What! would you be obliged in order to secure tranquillity of conscience to examine whether your confessor is learned or not ? It is sufficient that he is lawfully approved by his mission, which you may readily suppose ; from that moment he holds God's place to you, and you cannot be reprehensible in doing what he commands.

"But, perhaps, you will argue : I am not scrupulous ; my fears are not vain, but well founded. I reply, no insane person believes himself insane, for madness consists precisely in not recognizing that we have lost reason. Nevertheless I tell you you are scrupulous, you whom your director thinks so, because you will not recognize the vanity of your scruples ; if you understood that your apprehensions were vain you would pay no attention to them, and you would not be scrupulous. Then quiet yourself and obey your director, who knows your conscience.

"'That does not depend upon the director,' I hear you reply, 'but upon me, who cannot explain myself and make known to him the miserable state of my soul.'—Ah! there you are, inventing a thousand scruples on this head and making no scruple whatever of treating your spiritual father as an ignorant person, or one capable of sacrilege!

"For when you confessed your doubts, and upon grave matters, according to you the confessor, if he did not understand you, was obliged to put to you such questions as would enable him to judge of your doubts ; so that if without a just reason or without understanding you, as you think, he has ordered you to despise them as vain scruples, he must have done it through ignorance or negligence. Thus by distrusting his judgment through fear that he has not understood you, you represent him, as I said, either as ignorant or capable of sacrilege ; and you make no scruple of this rashness! Every one who permits herself to judge the decisions of confessors should be answered as the learned Bishop of Gubbio, Mgr. Sperelli, one day answered a scrupulous religious who denounced her confessor to him as a heretic because he had told her sins were not sins. 'Tell me, my daughter,' he said, 'in what university did you study theology that you know more than your confessor? Go busy yourself with spinning and cease to occupy yourself with these follies.'

"I would not say the same to you, but I urge you to abide tranquilly by all that your spiritual father tells you. It suffices that you have once exposed your doubts to him. Now and always, when he says, 'That is sufficient, I do not wish to hear any more, do as I tell you, go to communion,' etc., you should obey without another thought, and believe that he has understood you sufficiently; do not question the wisdom of his decision, but obey him blindly, without arguing, without seeking to know his motives, abandoning yourself completely to his guidance; for if you seek to know the reason of what he tells you, you will only awaken new scruples, and you will fall back into your perplexities. Obey blindly, that is, without pretending to discover the why or wherefore; and never set yourself to reflect upon what is prescribed you by your confessor. Scruples are like pitch, the more you handle them the more they stick to you ; the more you reflect upon them, the more involved you become. Be satisfied to walk in obscurity, bearing in mind the beautiful maxims of St. Francis de Sales, one of which is : 'We must be content to believe that we are doing well, on the word of a director and spiritual father, without seeking to know and feel it.' Another says : 'The best way is to walk blindly under the guidance of divine Providence through darkness, desolation, crosses and other perplexities of this life.' Another, finally, and this one should completely reassure you, says : 'A truly obedient soul is never lost.' Keep ever before your eyes this certain rule, that in obeying your confessor you obey God ; force yourself to obey without heeding your fears ; and be persuaded that if you do not obey, it is impossible for you to do well ; while, if you obey, you are always safe. Do not say then : and if I am lost in obeying, who will release me from hell?—For that is not possible. No ; it is not possible that obedience, which is the sure road to Paradise, should become for you the road to hell."

III.

Submission due to the Director.

"Obey your director and do not deviate from what he prescribes or permits you, however good anything contrary to his advice may seem. We read, in the lives of the early Fathers, that a young religious already far advanced in virtue willed, contrary to the advice of his spiritual father, to leave the monastery and retire into solitude. But what happened to him? From the desert, whither he had retired, he chose at one time to pay his parents a visit; while at home he forgot his solitude and abandoned himself to a lax life.

"You will tell me, perhaps, that following the guidance of your confessor you were very badly directed, as several priests have thus assured you.—I answer that you could hardly go astray in following the path of obedience. But if this did happen, do you know the reason? It was probably because you obeyed in certain things and not in others. God has not promised His concurrence to such defective obedience. Place yourself completely in the hands of your guide and obey him in all things; then God will never permit you to fall into error. If your confessor have not the necessary knowledge, God will take care to supply the deficiency, for it is not possible for a soul desiring to sanctify herself, and trusting in God, to be deceived when she faithfully obeys God's minister.

"Hence I conclude that a religious who has no particular director, cannot err in allowing herself to be directed by the ordinary confessor, though he be changed from time to time. A great servant of God, Sister Paula Centurion, used to say: 'To me all confessors seem the same; they all apply the Blood of Jesus Christ to heal the wounds of my soul.' When a new confessor comes, it suffices to give him a general knowledge of our conscience and thus place ourselves under his direction. To one who truly desires to sanctify herself, and seeks but God, every confessor assigned her by authority is good. We must have a good will, and a firm resolution to refuse self-love every satisfaction, to seek in all things only what is pleasing to God. For this reason the venerable Sister Ursula Benincasa used to say to her religious: 'Sisters, be persuaded that no director can lead you to sanctity, if you are not resolved to mortify your own will and your passions.'"

APPENDIX.

Two Letters of Marie Lataste.[*]

First Letter.

Necessity of a Director.

You asked me, whether the voice which spoke with me ever said anything to me of my director in a manner to found an instruction thereon? I have already answered you, yes.

The Saviour Jesus, for it seems to me to be really He who speaks to me, gave me several counsels as to how I should bear myself in my relations with my director. I

---

[*] " Independently of the marvellous communications of our Saviour with the humble Marie Lataste, we find in her writings such a breath of inspiration, such peace, such sweet simplicity, and deep unction, should they produce such an impression upon the soul, that in my opinion, the simple reading of the letters must lead us to discover God and His spirit in them.

" Several letters of Marie Lataste have been found singularly remarkable. We quote among others the first and second relative to the *necessity of having a director and the manner of conducting one's self toward him.*"

Etudes réligieuses par les PP. de la Compagnie de Jesus.

have referred to it in my note-books when I found occasion. But besides this He spoke to me in a most special manner of my director from the beginning when I had the happiness to hear His voice. He spoke to me three times in succession on this subject, and in the following order: First, on the necessity of a director; second, on how we bear ourselves in our relation with a director; third, on the qualities of a director.

I will give the first discourse, the necessity of a director:

"My daughter," said the Saviour Jesus to me one day after mass, "I have often recommended you to speak to him who directs you of what you experience in your relations with Me. You have never asked yourself the motive of this recommendation, nor, why you have not only a confessor but a director in him to whom you make known the secrets of your soul. I wish to make you understand and to show you how it is necessary it should be thus.

"Since the revolt of the first man all men are plunged in darkness; they have eyes, and yet they are incapable of guiding themselves in the way which leads to God. Life, in fact, is surrounded with dangers, perils, precipices; the enemies of man spring up everywhere in his path, and for this reason man needs other light than that of his eyes, or his intelligence, to be able to walk securely, and it is thus by the aid of directors and counsellors that all men must pursue their march to eternity.

"Such is the will of God. Man sinned through pride and willed to walk by his own light. He is punished in that in which he sinned, and until the end of ages man shall walk in the way of salvation by the light and guidance of another.

"You know how it has been since the beginning of the world. The heads of families were the counsellors of all the family, and as they could not find in their children the counsellors they needed themselves, God caused them to hear His voice and lent them His light and His counsel. Such were the heads of families, the patriarchs, the legislators, the prophets, and the pontiffs of the people of God. The counsels of these inspired men of God were the light and guidance of the people.

"When the time had come, I came Myself to be the universal Counsellor of the human race. I came to restore it light, truth, and life. I shed this light, this truth, and this life on my Apostles; and through the priesthood of those whom I have chosen as my ministers it passes to generations, enlightening intelligences, nourishing them with the only true food, vivifying them and leading them each day by a stronger, more generous life to the centre of that life which will never end.

"Therefore, man, My daughter, must make use of a counsellor or director because God has so regulated the commerce of the supernatural life.

"Behold man, My daughter, in the commerce of the natural life; he consults, he asks advice, counsel, light; be he the most learned, the most enlightened, the wisest of men, he distrusts himself, he has recourse to another.

"The supernatural life, with still stronger reason, requires that we act in like manner, if we would walk uprightly in this life, if we would not wander, or pursue a false path.

"You understand, in fact, that the supernatural life, my daughter, has an importance very different from the natural life, which is for time, while the other is for eternity. Therefore, if you examine the supernatural world, you will see all the saints, the greatest doctors, the doctor of nations himself, struck on the road to Damascus seeking of another counsel and light to walk in the way of God.

"I alone can dispense with counsel and light, for I am the counsel and the light of all; but all men are subjected to walk by the light of another and not by their own light and counsel.

"Men, the most learned, and the wisest in directing others, are like blind men who find themselves alone with no one to guide their steps, when they wish to walk according to their own wisdom. They grope blindly for awhile, they proceed slowly for a few days, and they fall into abysses. For man is blind to what concerns himself; he easily takes what is vicious and defective for goodness or virtue, and the error is to him the cause of a fall, or death. He falls because he has no one to guide him, he dies because he has not the assistance of a friend to withdraw him from a precipice. Therefore, if God, My daughter, has willed that all men should have a director, and if a director is a thing so necessary, that even without the express will of God all men should have one, you must see how important it is for you to be directed in the path of salvation by another guide than yourself.

"Yes, My daughter, you need a director that he may teach you that of which you are ignorant: the science of salvation, the science of the supernatural life. Though through kindness to you I have deigned to instruct you Myself, yet it is necessary that you submit my instructions to your director, that you may learn through him and know positively that you may receive My teachings and conform yourself thereto, for they contain nothing contrary to truth on the subject of your faith, your hope, your charity, and all the actions of your life. You fear to be the victim of illusions; who will reassure you on this point if not your director?

"You need a director that he may exercise you in the practice of all virtues, that he may indicate to you the means of avoiding sin, and that he may regulate your discretion in the fulfilment of your duties toward God.

"You need a director to increase your merits for eternity, and your crown in heaven, by your obedience and your submission to all that he prescribes. Obedience to his voice will give you greater resemblance to Me, who always did the will of My Father upon earth.

"You need a director, because life is full

of miseries, tribulations and trials; therefore you need a word of consolation in trial, succor to strengthen you in combat. And all this you find in your director.

" Finally, My daughter, you need a director because, like all the children of Adam, you are the victim of sin, inclined to evil, subject to offend God.

" Follow, then, the light, the counsels, the advice you receive from your director. Grieve not if I have taken from you him who first showed you the way. I tell you truly you will bless My Providence one day for having placed you in the hands of him whom I have sent to you."

Second Letter.

How to bear one's self toward a Director.

Here is the second discourse of the Saviour Jesus. He taught me, in this discourse, how I should bear myself toward my director.

"My daughter," He said, "I wish to teach you how you should act toward your director. There are two ways of acting for you, one interior, the other exterior; the first comprises the intimate sentiments of your soul, the second, your acts, and your exterior relations.

"What should be your exterior conduct in relation to your director?

"By what should it be regulated?

"My daughter, by sentiments of faith and religion.

"Your director is clothed with My priesthood, that is, with the greatest dignity that can possibly be communicated to man. He is a priest, he holds My place, he acts as I Myself would act, he has all My powers. You should consequently regard Me as living in his person; you should honor Me in honoring him, respect Me in respecting him; hear My voice in listening to him; submit to Me in submitting to him; you should feel for him the deepest and most sincere gratitude; you should love him as the spiritual father of your soul, as your guide, your counsellor, and your Saviour; for he fills for you the part of Saviour which I have assigned to him, as I have to all My priests.

"These sentiments should also be the rule of your exterior conduct.

"If you act with faith and piety, you will make yourself known to your director with simplicity, telling him all that you know, hiding nothing from him, communicating your secrets and the most intimate trials, you will speak to him as to God, whom you would not deceive, because He knows all things, even the most hidden thoughts; you will speak to him as to God, that is, as to your father, with confidence and freedom, hoping everything from him, and abandoning yourself to him with the conviction that he will act in the best way possible to enlighten you, to succor you, to help you in the combats or trials of life.

" You will submit your will to his as to Mine. You will not dispute with him; you will defer to his wisdom. You will be in his hands an instrument full of intelligence, to accomplish all that he prescribes.

" You are permitted, however, in certain cases, to humbly and deferentially represent an objection, but it must always be with the intention not to persist, but to act afterward according to the will of your director, when he shall have heard your objection.

" In acting thus, My daughter, your conduct will be irreproachable, your conduct will be full of merit, and you will obtain the recompense which I have promised to those who hear My word, I will come to you and I will make My abode with you."

It was thus the Saviour Jesus told me to act toward my director.

I do not know whether I have acted thus in all circumstances ; but my most earnest desire is always to conform myself to this teaching.

Yes, I wish to submit in all things to what it will please you to counsel or command me. I wish to have no other will but yours.

In regard to the frankness or simplicity with which I make known to you all that passes within me, I assure you that my serious intention is to conceal nothing from you, and if I do not tell you all, it is because I have forgotten it.

‘Epistle of St. Ignatius on Obedience.

" Ignatius of Loyola to the Brethren of the Society of Jesus who are in Portugal, wishes grace and love everlasting in Christ our Lord.

" 1. It is a cause of great comfort to me, most dear Brethren in Christ, when I hear it reported with what earnest desire and endeavor you strive to attain to the highest perfection of all virtue and piety, by His favor Who, as He has called you to this kind of life, so in His mercy keeps you in the same, and directs you to that blessed end whereunto those that are chosen by Him do arrive.

---

* We reproduce here this beautiful letter of St. Ignatius as we find it in the Book of Rules of the Society of Jesus.
 Being little known in communities, we have thought proper to add it to our work. Ponder it well, and it will cause you to appreciate " SPIRITUAL DIRECTION," which is simply the submission of our judgment and our will to the judgment and will of a person who holds God's place to us, and to whom God Himself has said : " He that heareth you heareth Me, and he that despiseth you despiseth Me. "

"2. And truly, though I wish you to be perfect in all spiritual gifts and ornaments, yet especially do I desire (as you have understood of me heretofore) to see you most eminent in the virtue of Obedience ; and this not only for the excellent and singular fruits thereof which are proved by many testimonies of Holy Writ, and by examples both in the Old and New Testament; but also because as St. Gregory (L. 35, c. 10) says : 'Obedience is the only virtue that plants all other virtues in the mind, and preserves them after they are once planted.' As long as this virtue shall flourish, all others doubtless will flourish and bring forth such fruits in your hearts as I desire and He, with good reason, requires ; Who, by His salutary obedience, redeemed mankind when afflicted and destroyed through the crime of disobedience, becoming obedient unto death, even to the death of the cross.—Philip. ii, 8.

"3. More easily may we suffer ourselves to be surpassed by other Religious Orders in fasting, watching, and other severities in diet and apparel, which, according to their institute and rule, every one of them does piously practice ; but in true and perfect Obedience and the abnegation of our will and judgment, I greatly desire, most dear brethren, that those who serve God in this Society should be conspicuous, and that the true and genuine progeny of the same should, as it were, be distinguished by this mark, that they regard not the individual whom they obey, but in him, Christ our Lord, for whose love they obey. For the Superior is not to be obeyed because he is prudent, or virtuous, or excels in any other divine gift, whatsoever it be ; but for this only, that he is in the place of God, and has authority from Him who says : 'He that heareth you heareth Me ; and he that despiseth you despiseth Me.' —Luke x, 16. Neither, on the other hand, if he be wanting in understanding or prudence, is he therefore to be the less obeyed in that wherein he is Superior ; since he represents Him Whose Wisdom cannot be deceived, and Who will supply whatsoever shall be wanting in His substitute, whether it be virtue or other qualities. Wherefore, Christ our Lord, when He had said in express and open terms : ' The Scribes and Pharisees have sitten upon the chair of Moses ;' presently added : ' all things therefore whatsoever they shall say to you, observe and do ; but according to their works do ye not.'—St. Matt. xxiii, 2.

" 4. Wherefore I desire that you should earnestly endeavor with all care and diligence to acknowledge CHRIST in every Superior, and with great devotion, reverence and obey in him the divine Majesty. This will seem to you less strange, if you consider how the Apostle St. Paul commands us to obey even secular Superiors and Gentiles as Christ Himself, from whom all well-ordered authority is derived, for thus he writes to the Ephesians : ' Be obedient to them that are your temporal lords according to the flesh, with fear and trembling, in the simplicity of your heart, as to Christ, not serving to the eye as it were pleasing men; but as the servants of Christ, doing the will of God from the heart ; with a good will serving as to the Lord and not to men.' And from this you yourself may judge what account in his heart a religious man ought to make of his Superior to whom he has given himself to be ruled and governed, not only as to a Superior, but expressly as to one that has the place of CHRIST :— whether he should look on him as man, or as the Vicar of CHRIST.

"5. Moreover, I desire that this should be thoroughly understood and deeply imprinted in your minds that it is but a base and very imperfect kind of Obedience which consists in the external execution only of that which is commanded ; and that it is not worthy of the name of virtue, unless it pass to a further degree, making the will of the Superior our will, and so agreeing with the same that not only is there external fulfilment of the command, but also agreement of will ; that so both may be of one mind in willing and not willing the same. And for this reason it is said in Holy Writ : 'Obedience is better than sacrifices.' — 1 Kings xv, 22. For as St. Gregory teaches us, ' In victims, the flesh of another, but in obedience, our own will is killed.' And because this part of the soul is so excellent, hence it is that the offering of it to our Lord and Creator, through Obedience, is of great price and value.

"6. It is then a very great and dangerous mistake, not only in those who imagine that they are not obliged to obey in things appertaining to flesh and blood, but also in those who persuade themselves that they can deviate from the will of the Superior in things otherwise very holy and spiritual, as fasting, prayer, or other good works. Let them give ear to what Cassian prudently remarks in the conference of Daniel the Abbot, saying : 'It is one and the self-same kind of disobedience, whether in earnestness of labor, or from desire of ease, one breaks the command of the Superior, and as prejudicial to go against the statutes of the Monastery out of sloth, as out of watchfulness; and finally, it is as much to transgress the precept of the Abbot by reading, as to contemn it by sleeping.' Holy was the action of Martha, holy the contemplation of Mary Magdalen, and holy the penance and tears wherewith she watered the feet of CHRIST our Lord; but all this was to be done in Bethania, which word is interpreted, the house of Obedience, whereby our Lord would signify to us, as St. Bernard says, that 'neither the endeavor of good works, nor the quiet of contemplation, nor the tears of the penitent, could have been grateful unto Him out of Bethania.'*

"7. Wherefore, most dear Brethren, cast off wholly, as far as you can, your own wills: deliver freely, and dedicate to your Creator in His substitute, the freedom He has bestowed upon you. Consider it no little advantage of your free will that you are able to give it back fully, through Obedience, to Him from whom you received it And by so doing you not only do not lose the same, but rather increase and perfect it; since by this means you direct all your wills by that

---

* Serm. ad Milit. Templ. c. 13.

most certain rule of rectitude, the will of God interpreted unto you by him who in place of God governs you.

"8. And for this reason, you must always be very careful that you never seek to wrest the Superior's will (which you ought to hold for the will of God Himself) unto your own: for this would be, not to conform your will unto God's, but to endeavor to rule His will by yours, inverting the order of His Divine Wisdom. Oh! how great an error it is, and one which belongs to such as self-love has blinded, to account themselves obedient, when by some means or other they have brought the Superior to that which they desire. Listen to St. Bernard, a man eminently experienced in this matter : 'Whosoever,' says he, 'endeavors either openly or covertly to have his spiritual Father enjoin him what he himself desires, deceives himself, if he flatters himself that he is a true follower of obedience ; for in that he does not obey his Superior, but rather the Superior obeys him'.* It follows, therefore, that whosoever is desirous of the virtue of Obedience must necessarily attain to this second degree so as not only to fulfil the Superior's

---

*Serm. de trib. Ordin. Eccl.

command, but to make also the Superior's will his own will, or rather, to put off his own will, that he may put on the will of God declared to him by his Superior.

"9. But he that will wholly sacrifice himself to God, besides his will, must also offer up his understanding (which is the third and highest degree of obedience); that he may not only will but also think the self-same with his Superior; and submit his own judgment unto him, so far as a devout will can bend the understanding. For though this power of the soul has that freedom wherewith the will is endowed, and by nature itself is drawn to assent to whatsoever is represented unto it as true, yet nevertheless, in many things, in which the evidence of the known truth does not force it, it may, by the strength of the will, be inclined more one way than another. When these things happen, whosoever professes Obedience must submit himself to the judgment of the Superior. For obedience, being a holocaust, in which the whole man, nothing at all excepted, is offered up unto his Creator and Lord in the fire of charity through the hands of his substitute, and as it is also a full renunciation, in which a religious man freely yields up all his own rights to dedicate and bind himself to God, to be possessed and governed by His divine Providence by means of his Superior; it cannot be denied that Obedience comprehends not only the execution, so that the person do that which is commanded, and the will, so that he do it willingly, but also the judgment, that whatsoever the Superior commands and thinks good, seem just and reasonable to the inferior, so far, as I have said, as the will by its force and vigor can bend the understanding.

"10. Would that this obedience of the understanding and judgment were as much understood and put in practice by men, as it is grateful to God, and necessary for all those who live in Religion. For as in the celestial bodies and globes, to the end that one may receive motion and influence from the other, it is necessary that, with certain conformity and order, the inferior globe be subject to the superior; so amongst men, when one is moved by another's authority (as happens in obedience) it is necessary that he who depends upon another be subject and subordinate, to the end that he may receive some virtue and influence from him who commands. Now this kind of subjection and obedience can in no wise stand unless the will and judgment of the inferior agree with the will and judgment of the Superior.

"11. Moreover, if we regard the end and intention of Obedience as our will, so our judgment may be deceived as to what is good to us; wherefore if, lest our will should stray, we conform it to the will of the Superior, our understanding is also to be ruled by his, to the end it may not err: 'Lean not upon thy own prudence,'—Prov. iii, 5,—says the Holy Scripture. And even, in worldly matters, those who are wise, judge it to be the part of a prudent man not to trust his own wisdom, especially in his own cause, in which, when the mind is troubled, one can hardly be a good judge. And if, in matters concerning ourselves, we are to prefer the judgment and counsel of another, who is not our own Superior, before our own, how much more the counsel and judgment of the Superior to whom we have yielded ourselves to be directed, as to one who is in place of God and interpreter of His divine will. And certain it is that in spiritual matters and persons, so much the more heed is to be taken, as the danger of a spiritual course is greater when one runs along therein without the bridle of counsel and discretion. Wherefore Cassian, in the conference of Abbot Moses, says: 'By no other way does the devil draw a monk headlong and bring him to death sooner, than by persuading him to neglect the counsel of the Elders and trust to his own judgment and determination.' (Coll. ii, 11.)

"12. Moreover, unless we have this Obedience of our understanding, it is impossible that either the consent of our will or the execution, will be such as they ought to be, for nature itself has so ordained that the concupiscible power of the soul must follow the apprehensive, and the will without violence cannot long obey against the understanding. And if there be any who for some time obey, induced by that common apprehension, that obey they must, though commanded amiss, yet doubtless this cannot be firm and constant, and so perseverance fails, or at least the perfection of Obedience which consists in obeying promptly and with alacrity, for, there can be no alacrity and diligence where there is discord of minds and opinions. Then perish that zeal and speed in performing, when we doubt whether it be expedient or not to do what we are commanded; then perishes that renowned simplicity of blind obedience, when we call, in question the justice of the command, and perhaps, even we condemn the Superior, because he bids us to do such things as are not very pleasing unto us : then fails humility ; for although on the one hand we obey, yet on the other we prefer ourselves before our Superior, then fails fortitude in difficult enterprises, and (to conclude in brief) the whole force and dignity of this virtue are lost. And in place thereof, there arise pain, trouble, reluctance, weariness, murmurings, excuses and other vices of no small moment, by which the value and merit of Obedience are wholly destroyed. Wherefore St. Bernard, of those who take it ill when things are enjoined that seem somewhat hard unto them, speaks as follows : 'If you begin to grieve at this, to judge your Superior, to murmur in your heart, though outwardly you fulfil what is commanded, yet this is not the virtue of patience, but a cloak of your malice.'* And if peace and tranquillity of mind are desired, he certainly shall never acquire them who has within himself the cause of his disquiet and trouble, to wit, the disagreeing of his own judgment from the law of Obedience.

---

* Serm. 3, de Circumcis.

"13. And therefore, for the maintaining of union, which is the bond of every society, the Apostle so earnestly exhorts all* to think and say the same thing, that by the agreeing of their wills and judgments they may be mutually comforted and sustained. Now, if there must be one and the self-same sentiment between the members and the head, you may easily judge whether it is more just that the head should yield to the members or the members unto the head. It is plain then, by what has hitherto been said, that this obedience of the understanding is necessary.

"14. But how perfect the same is in itself and how pleasing to God, we may gather by this : First, because thereby the most excellent and precious part of man is consecrated unto Him : secondly, because the obedient man is by this means made a living holocaust most grateful to His Divine Majesty, keeping nothing whatever to himself : lastly, by reason of the great difficulty of the combat ; for the obedient man overcomes himself for the love of God, and resists that natural inclination which all men have to embrace and follow their own opinions. Hence, therefore, it follows that Obedience, though its proper fruit seems to be to perfect the will, in-

---
* Rom. xv. 5l. 1 Cor. i, 10. 2.Cor. xxii, 11. Philip, ii, 2.

asmuch as it makes it prompt and ready at the beck of the Superior, yet it must belong also to the understanding, as we have declared, and bring it to be of the self-same opinion in all things with the Superior, that all the forces of the will and understanding being united together, we may fulfil what is commanded with all speed and integrity.

"15. It seems to me, most dear brethren, I hear you say, that you now no longer doubt of the necessity of this virtue, but that you earnestly desire to know how you may attain to the perfection thereof. To this question I answer with St. Leo: 'Nothing is difficult unto the humble, and nothing hard unto the meek:' so that if you want not humility nor mildness, assuredly God will not be wanting in His goodness to help you to perform that which you have promised Him, not only patiently but also willingly.

"16. Moreover, three things I will lay down unto you, which will greatly further you in the attainment of this obedience of your understanding. The first is, that, as I said in the beginning, you do not behold in the person of your Superior a man subject to errors, and miseries, but CHRIST Himself, Who is the highest Wisdom, Immeasur-

Epistle of St. Ignatius on Obedience. 259

able Goodness, and Infinite Charity, who neither can be deceived, nor will deceive you. And because you are conscious within yourselves that you have undergone this yoke of Obedience for the love of God, to the end that you might, in following the Superior's will, more assuredly follow the Divine Will, doubt not but the most faithful charity of our Lord continually directs you, and leads you the right way, by the hands of those whom He has given you for Superiors. Wherefore, hear their voice, no otherwise than if it were the voice of Christ, seeing that the Apostle, writing to the Colossians and exhorting subjects to obey their lords, says as follows : 'Whatsoever you do, do it from the heart, as to the Lord and not to man, knowing that you shall receive of the Lord the reward of inheritance ; serve ye the Lord Christ.'* And St. Bernard, ' Whether God, or man His substitute, commands anything, we must obey with equal diligence, and perform it with like reverence, when, however, man commands nothing that is contrary to God.'† And thus if you do not look upon man with the eyes of the body, but upon God with those of the soul, it

---
*Col. iii. 23.
†Tract. de Praecep. and Dispen. C. xii.

will certainly be hard to conform your will and judgment to that rule which you yourselves have chosen.

"17. Another means is that you always seriously endeavor to defend within yourselves, that which your Superior commands or thinks good, but never to disapprove of it. And to this it will help to be well affected towards whatsoever he shall command; whereby you shall not only obey without trouble, but even with joy and pleasure. For as St. Leo says, 'It is not hard to serve where we love that which is commanded.'*

"18. The last means to subject your understanding both more easily and securely, and also in use among the holy Fathers, is to determine within yourselves whatsoever the Superior commands, to be the commandment and will of Almighty God Himself; and as in order to believe what the Catholic Faith proposes, you at once bend all the forces of your mind to consent thereunto, so in doing that which your Superior commands, you must be carried with a kind of blind impulse of your will desirous to obey. So it is thought Abraham did when he was ordered to sacrifice his son Isaac; † so, under

---

* Serm. 4 de jejun sep. mensis.
† Gen. xxii.

the new law, did some of those holy Fathers whom Cassian speaks of, as John the Abbot,* who did not question whether that which he was commanded to do was profitable or not, as when, with such great and continued labor, for a year together he watered a dry stick ; nor whether it could be done or not, as when he endeavored so earnestly to move a huge rock, which many men together could not have stirred.

This kind of Obedience we see sometimes confirmed by miracle. For, to say nothing of others, whom you yourselves are not ignorant of, Maurus, St. Benedict's disciple,† going by command of his Superior into a lake, did not sink. Another being bid by his Superior to bring a lioness to him, took hold of her and brought her unto him.

Wherefore this manner of subjecting our own judgment so as, without questioning, to sanction and approve within ourselves whatever the Superior commands, is not only a common practice among holy men, but also to be imitated by all who are desirous of perfect Obedience in all things, in which manifestly there appears no sin.

" 19. Neither are you hindered by this, if

---

* L. 4. C. xxxiv and xvi.
† Greg. 2 Dial. C. vii.

anything occurs to you different from the Superior's opinion, and it seems (after you have commended the same humbly to God) that it ought to be declared, from proposing it unto him : wherein lest self-love and your own judgment should deceive you, this precaution is to be taken, that you remain most indifferent, before and after you have made the proposition, not only as to undertaking or relinquishing the matter of which there is question, but also as to approving and thinking better whatsoever seems good to the Superior.

"20. And this which I have said of Obedience, is equally to be observed by every private person towards his immediate Superior, and by the Rectors and local Superiors towards the Provincials and by the Provincials towards the General and by the General towards him whom God has placed over him, to wit, His Vicar upon earth ; to the end that thus a perfect distinction of degrees, and consequently peace and charity, may be preserved ; without which the right of government, neither of our Society, nor of any other congregation can be maintained. And this kind of proceeding the Divine Providence uses, in disposing all things sweetly, and bringing them to their appointed ends, the lowest by the middlemost, and the middlemost by the highest. Whence also flows that subordination in Angels of one Choir towards another, and that perfect harmony of the celestial bodies and all things which are moved, each in its own determined place and position, whose resolutions and motions proceed orderly from one Supreme mover by degrees unto the lowest. The same we see upon earth, as well in all well-ordered commonwealths, as most of all in the Ecclesiastical Hierarchy, whose members and functions are all derived from one General Vicar of Christ our Lord ; and, by how much the more exactly this disposition and order are kept, by so much the whole government is better ; and on the other hand, by the neglect hereof, what grievous damages have befallen various Congregations, there is no one who does not see. And therefore, in this Society whereof our Lord has delivered unto me some charge and care, I desire that this virtue should be practised as diligently and flourish as perfectly, as if the whole good and safety of our Society depended hereon.

"21. Wherefore, that where my epistle began, there it may also end, I most earnestly beseech you for Christ our **Lord's** sake

Who gave Himself unto us not only as a Master but as an example of Obedience, that you will bend all your forces to the attaining of this virtue; and that desirous and greedy of so glorious a victory, you will endeavor to overcome yourselves, that is, to conquer and subdue the most excellent and difficult part of your soul, your will, I say, and understanding; and to the end that the true and solid knowledge and love of God Almighty our Lord may draw you wholly unto Him, and rule and govern you in the whole course of this life and pilgrimage, until at length He bring you, and many others assisted by your help and example, to the last and most happy end of bliss everlasting.

"I commend myself most earnestly to God in your prayers.

"*From Rome, the 26th of March,* 1553."

THE Catholic Family Library.

The Christian Father; What he should be, and what he should do. With Prayers suitable to his condition. From the German by Rev. L. A. Lambert, Waterloo, N. Y. With an Introduction by Rt. Rev. S. V. RYAN, D.D., C.M., Bishop of Buffalo. **Fifth Edition.**
Paper, 25 cts.; Maroquette, 35 cts.; Cloth, 50 cts.; French Mor. flex., red edges, $1.00.

The Christian Mother; The Education of her Children and her Prayer. Translated by a Father of the Society of Jesus. **Ninth Edition.** With an Introduction by the Most Rev. JAMES GIBBONS, D.D., Archbishop of Baltimore.
Paper, 25 cts.; Maroquette, 35 cts.; Cloth, 50 cts.; French Mor. flex., red edges, $1.00

A Sure Way to a Happy Marriage.
A Book of Instructions for those Betrothed and for Married People. Translated by Rev. Edward I. Taylor. **Third Edition Revised.**
Paper, 30 cts.; Maroquette, 40 cts.; Cloth, 60 cts.

In token of my appreciation, I request you to forward me **A thousand (1000) copies** of each of the two former books and **five hundred (500)** of the third for distribution among my people. Yours faithfully in Christ,
✠ JAMES VINCENT CLEARY, *Bishop of Kingston.*

From the Pastoral Letters of Right Rev. M. J. O'FARRELL, D.D., Bishop of Trenton.

"For Parents we recommend 'THE CHRISTIAN FATHER' and 'THE CHRISTIAN MOTHER,' in which they will fully learn all their duties to their children."—*Pastoral*, 1883.

"We **strongly recommend for your perusal and serious consideration** two little books lately published: one is entitled 'A SURE WAY TO A HAPPY MARRIAGE,' and the other 'An Instruction on Mixed Marriages,' by the Right Rev. Dr. Ullathorne."—*Pastoral*, 1882.

BENZIGER BROTHERS, New York, Cincinnati and St. Louis.

THE
Truths of Salvation.

BY REV. J. PERGMAYR, S.J.

TRANSLATED FROM THE GERMAN BY A FATHER OF THE SAME SOCIETY. WITH THE PERMISSION OF SUPERIORS.

16mo, cloth. $1.00.

———o———

The basis of this work is "The Spiritual Exercises of St. Ignatius." The original is used as a book of Meditations, and also for retreats in nearly every Convent in Germany. Though written for those living in religious communities it will be found equally useful for Christians in the world, as it is offered to all who earnestly desire to consider the truths of salvation, and to acquire self-knowledge.

To those unaccustomed to meditate, or others who, from weakness or indisposition, are incapable of mental application, it will prove an efficient aid.

Solid Virtue:
A TRIDUUM AND SPIRITUAL CONFERENCES.

BY REV. FATHER BELLECIUS, S.J.

Translated from the original Latin, by a Father of the Society of Jesus. With the permission of Superiors.

16mo, cloth. 75 cents.

This is a translation of Fr. Bellecius's own abridgment of his larger work on Solid Virtue. It tells us in simplest language of all that goes to constitute genuine devotion, or solid virtue, how it may be practically acquired, what prevents many from attaining it, and how fruitful of choicest grace and happiness it is when attained. It is a book destined to advance numerous souls steadily on the path to Christian perfection, and generally to produce wide-spread and abiding good in the cloister, within the Sanctuary, and among lay Catholic people.

BENZIGER BROTHERS, New York, Cincinnati, and St. Louis.

Sent free by mail, on receipt of price.

THE
True Spouse of Christ;
OR,
The Nun Sanctified by the Virtues of her State.

By ST. ALPHONSUS M. LIGUORI,

Translated from the Italian

BY THE VERY REV. DR. CALLAN.

481 pages, crown octavo, cloth, $1.50

In his Introduction to the book, the Saintly Author says:

" This work, as appears from the title, is intended particularly for Nuns. However, only a small portion of it is directed exclusively to them ; the remainder, but especially what regards the observance of the vows of religion, regular discipline, and the perfection of the religious state, is equally suited to religious of all denominations ; and what regards the Christian virtues will be found highly useful even for seculars.

" To each chapter I have annexed prayers, replete with pious affections, knowing that such prayers are very acceptable to religious who seek perfection."

A Much Needed Work !

The Sunday-School Teacher's Manual.

BY REV. A. A. LAMBING,

AUTHOR OF "THE ORPHAN'S FRIEND," ETC., ETC.

16mo, 216 pages, cloth, 75 cts.

Published with the Approbation of his Eminence the Cardinal Archbishop of New York and of the Author's Ordinary.

BENZIGER BROTHERS, New York, Cincinnati, and St. Louis.

GOLDEN SANDS.
THIRD SERIES.
TRANSLATED FROM THE FRENCH
By Miss ELLA McMAHON
32mo, cloth. 60 cents.

"I love these little messengers of God, one alone sometimes does more for me than a missionary."—**Pius IX.** to the Author of "Golden Sands."

"The practice of the little virtues, as St. Francis de Sales calls them, sanctifies daily life; and we know of no book, which insinuates these little virtues, more successfully than "Golden Sands."—*Ave Maria.*

"Rich in practical suggestions for the sanctification of daily duties."—*Catholic Mirror.*

"We hope the book will find its way into many Catholic houses and be the means of keeping the minds of Catholic children free from contamination of any kind."—*Connecticut Catholic.*

"Open the book anywhere, and you find a jewel of consolation, or explanation, or advice."—*Western Home Journal.*

"The work is small, but the beautiful counsels, and admonitions contained in it are great, and worthy of being stored in memory's store-house by every man, women, and child."—Pittsburg *Catholic.*

"Contains the very essence of the most profound thoughts told in the simplest and most charming style."—*Catholic Herald.*

"A collection of little counsels for the sanctification and happiness of daily life, and is a book which should be put in the hands of every young person."— New York *Sunday Union.*

"A book that can be opened at any page and read with profit. Its counsels heeded, would lead to happiness."— The Bay City, Mich., *Catholic Chronicle.*

"It is filled with good counsels, and no one can peruse it without benefit."—Richmond, Va., *Catholic Visitor.*

"Whatever may be one's failing or misery, strength and consolation can be found in the beautiful doctrines contained in this treasure."—Cleveland *Catholic Knight.*

BENZIGER BROTHERS, New York, Cincinnati, and St. Louis.

A BOOK FOR THE FAMILY!

GOFFINE'S
DEVOUT INSTRUCTIONS
ON THE EPISTLES AND GOSPELS.

For the Sundays and Holidays; with Explanations of Christian Faith and Duty and of Church Ceremonies. By the REV. LEONARD GOFFINE. Translated by the REV. THEO. NOETHEN.

Crown 8vo. Cloth, ink and gold side. Frontispiece. $1.50.

As a work of spiritual reading and instruction GOFFINE'S DEVOUT INSTRUCTIONS stands in the foremost rank. In it the faithful will find explained in a plain, simple manner the doctrines of the Church, her sacraments and ceremonies, as set forth in the Epistles and Gospels of the Sundays and holy days. The Catholic Church has at all times joined instruction with the offering of the Holy Sacrifice. But as the words of the speaker pass away and are forgotten, it is proper that preaching and spiritual reading should support each other. By this means instruction is more deeply impressed on the heart, and much that we might lose by neglect may thus be preserved. For these reasons, the reading of spiritual books is recommended as a means of properly keeping Sundays and holy days.

By the help of this book, those who are prevented by just cause from assisting at Mass may be enabled to arrange their family devotions. In Europe, the original of GOFFINE'S INSTRUCTIONS is extensively used for this purpose, and it is not only recommended and circulated there by the Bishops and priests, but some of the most learned and distinguished German divines have from time to time edited it.

The translator of the present Edition, which is undoubtedly **the best English version,** has not restricted himself to the text of any one Edition, but has made use of several of those that are most esteemed.

BENZIGER BROTHERS, New York, Cincinnati, and St. Louis.

NEW, ENLARGED EDITION.

Hours Before the Altar;

OR,

Meditations on the Holy Eucharist.

By MGR. DE LA BOUILLERIE,
Coadjutor Bishop of Bordeaux.

*Translated and Enlarged from the Fifty-First French Edition
By a Sister of Mercy.*

32mo, Cloth, - - 50 Cents.

These meditations which have passed through fifty-one editions in France are addressed to those pious souls who have tasted the sweetness of the Lord in the Sacrament of the Altar. They are published in the hope that they will suggest a method of meditating on the sweet mystery of the Most Blessed Sacrament, and that they may prove like those feeble lamps suspended before our Sanctuaries, which give light enough to guide our steps to the Tabernacle, but not enough to diminish the charm of its mysterious darkness, coming thus as an aid to prayer, but without taking from its recollection.

A Thought of St. Teresa's

FOR EVERY DAY IN THE YEAR.

Translated from the French by Miss ELLA McMAHON.

32mo, Extra Cloth, 50 Cents.

This little book contains the **most precious thoughts** of one of the greatest mystic writers of the Church.

In it the pious soul will find prayerful suggestions, food for meditation, and consoling words in time of affliction. Short and to the point, these **thoughts** will be recurred to daily, and it is hoped may soon become familiar to the lips of American Catholics.

BENZIGER BROTHERS, New York, Cincinnati, and St. Louis.

Souvenir of the Novitiate.

Especially intended for the use of Religious Communities devoted to the Education of Youth.

TRANSLATED FROM THE FRENCH BY

REV. EDWARD I. TAYLOR.

Published with the approbation of the Translator's Ordinary and of His Eminence the Cardinal, Archbishop of New York.
32mo, 285 pages, cloth, ink and gold side, red edges, $1.

Paradise on Earth

OPENED TO ALL;

OR,

A RELIGIOUS VOCATION

THE SUREST WAY IN LIFE.

Translated from the Italian of Rev. ANTONIO NATALE, S.J.
32mo, 146 pages, cloth, gold and inked side, red edges, 60 cents.

BENZIGER BROTHERS, New York, Cincinnati, and St. Louis

Sent free by mail on receipt of price.

NEW PRACTICAL MEDITATIONS
FOR EVERY DAY IN THE YEAR,
ON THE LIFE OF OUR LORD JESUS CHRIST.

Chiefly intended for the Use of Religious Communities.

By the Rev. Father BRUNO VERCRUYSSE, S.J.

The only complete English translation. Published with the approbation and under the direction of the author.

Enriched by several Novenas and Octaves; Meditations for the First Friday of every month and for the Days of Communion; Exercises preparatory to the Renewal of Vows, and for a Retreat of Eight Days; a New Method of Hearing Mass, and Practical Remarks on the Different Parts of Meditations; a Plan of Jerusalem, with a Map of Palestine, showing the different Localities mentioned throughout the Work, and an Alphabetical Table of Contents and of Meditations on the Gospels of the Sundays.

2 vols., 1244 pp. Extra cloth, bevelled boards, red edges. $5.

The merit of this work is established by the many editions through which it has passed—no less than 19,000 copies having been printed in different languages, within six years—as also, by the approbations it has received from the ecclesiastical authorities and from the SUPERIOR-GENERAL OF THE SOCIETY OF JESUS.

The Meditations are short but thoroughly practical, and will be found invaluable to the Reverend Clergy, as they furnish ample material for homilies on the Gospels and for sermons on the feasts of the year, and the principal points of morals. The feasts of the several founders of religious orders are in the second volume arranged according to their dates.

A PRAYER BEFORE MEDITATION and some admirable REMARKS ON THE CONSIDERATIONS are printed separately, on a loose sheet of heavy paper, and accompany each volume, serving the purpose of a book-mark.

In connection with the above, we have issued an excellent

METHOD OF HEARING MASS,

of a form suitable for inserting in prayer-books. It is extensively circulated in Europe, in the academies and colleges. Price, 50 cents per 100.

BENZIGER BROTHERS, New York, Cincinnati, and St. Louis.

SENT FREE BY MAIL, ON RECEIPT OF PRICE.

PEARLS FROM THE CASKET

OF THE

SACRED HEART OF JESUS.

A COLLECTION OF THE

Letters, Maxims, and Practices

OF THE

Blessed Margaret Mary Alacoque,

RELIGIOUS OF THE ORDER OF THE VISITATION.

EDITED BY

ELEANOR C. DONNELLY.

"*I constitute thee heir of My Heart, and of all Its treasures for time and eternity, permitting thee to use them according to thy desire. I promise thee that thou shalt never want assistance until I shall fail in power. Thou shalt be forever Its beloved disciple, the delight of Its predilection, and the holocaust of Its love.*"—WORDS OF OUR LORD TO BLESSED MARGARET MARY.

32mo, 192 pages.   Cloth, red edges, gilt side, 50 cents.

BENZIGER BROTHERS, New York, Cincinnati, and St. Louis.

Sent free by mail, on receipt of price.

THE IMITATION
OF THE
Sacred Heart of Jesus.

BY REV. F. ARNOUDT, S.J.

TRANSLATED FROM THE LATIN OF REV. J. M. FASTRE.

12mo, 798 pages, extra cloth, $2.00.

This delightful book contains ample matter for daily meditation throughout the year. The reader can start from the beginning and continue to the end of the work, or he may break this order and confine himself to such portions as are specially adapted to his feelings at the time. Things are not proposed here in general and in common, as is usually done in books of meditation, but everything is laid down specially and in particular, both in regard to the evil to be avoided, and the good to be practiced. The book greatly resembles the "Imitation of Christ," to which it is a fitting companion, but it is more regular in plan, more complete, actual, definite. The style of the work is everywhere suited to the subject, and the diction is pure

---

The Hidden Treasure;
OR, THE VALUE AND EXCELLENCE OF
THE HOLY MASS.
WITH A
Practical and Devout Method of Hearing it with Profit.

BY THE BLESSED LEONARD OF PORT-MAURICE.

18mo, 188 pages, cloth, 40 cents.

BENZIGER BROTHERS, New York, Cincinnati, and St. Louis.

Names That Live

IN CATHOLIC HEARTS:

Memoirs of Cardinal Ximenes—Michael Angelo—Samuel de Champlain—Archbishop Plunkett—Charles Carroll —Henri Larochejacquelein—Simon de Montfort.

By Miss ANNA T. SADLIER.

12mo, cloth, $1.00.

"A book **worth reading and keeping to read over again**. It is good for us to be told of the illustrious dead who were loyal to the Mother Church—the long line of Saints, Sages, Statesmen, Explorers and Scientists, who with all their greatness, were as little children at the footstool of God; and in this book we are reminded of some of these heroes to whom fame has builded a monument more enduring than brass, but whose highest claim to our admiration is the virtue which has placed an aureola of glory about their brow."—*Catholic Mirror.*

" **No more delightful reading can be placed in the hands of young people, or even adults,** than this volume of Biographical Essays."—*The Pilot.*

" Each of these delightful memoirs is a prose poem written in faultless style, fair and beautiful as a painting by a master hand inserted in a jeweled setting of great value."—Lawrence, Mass., *Catholic Herald.*

" Every word in it is **calculated to lift the reader's heart nearer to truth, holiness and heroism.**"—*Morning Star.*

" The lives of such men as these—whose characters were formed on true models—will remind the reader that he can make his life sublime in the best sense."—*Western Home Journal.*

" The lives of the great Catholic heroes it embraces are brought before us in graphic, living words, and **leave on our minds a pleasing and interesting picture.**"—*N. Y. Tablet.*

" Miss Sadlier paints her pictures in brilliant colors, and while she preserves the accuracy of the historian, glows with the enthusiasm of the poet."—*Donahoe's Magazine.*

" The sketches are written by Miss Anna T. Sadlier **in that lady's usual excellent style.**"—*Connecticut Catholic.*

" **Very attractive and interesting,** and must necessarily please the reader."—*Catholic Visitor.*

BENZIGER BROTHERS, New York, Cincinnati, and St. Louis.

THE YOUNG GIRL'S
BOOK OF PIETY
AT SCHOOL AND AT HOME.

A Prayer-Book for Girls in Convent-Schools and Academies,

BY

The Author of "Golden Sands."

TRANSLATED FROM THE 45th FRENCH EDITION.

Honored with a Blessing from the late POPE PIUS IX., and approved by many Archbishops and Bishops.

No.
4126, Cloth................................. $ .80
4136, French morocco, gilt centre and edges......... 1.35
4136½,   "   "   "   "   clasp......... 1.60
4147, Turkey morocco, antique, extra, gilt centre
   and edges.................................... 3.25
4147½, Turkey morocco, antique, extra, gilt centre
   and edges and clasp 3.75
4152, Calf, antique, edges red under gold........... 3.50
4158, Silk velvet, rim and clasp, gilt edges, orn. centre 6.00
4161,   "   "   "   "   "   rich ornaments 8.00

The Reverend author of this Prayer-book, for many years Spiritual Director of a Young Ladies' Academy, and who has devoted the best years of his life to the preparation of books of instruction for female youth, in this volume places his vast experience of human nature at the service of young girls in Convent-schools and Academies. The result is a book which embraces all that is essential for forming their tender hearts to piety and guiding their footsteps in the sure path of virtue. Written at the suggestion of a truly Christian heart, it breathes, from first to last, a perfume of sweet piety and of grace which often recalls the writings of St. Francis de Sales.

BENZIGER BROTHERS, New York, Cincinnati, and St. Louis.

The Imitation of Christ.

By THOMAS A KEMPIS. In four books. Translated from the original Latin by the Right Rev. RICHARD CHALLONER, D.D.
13mo, 481 pages. Printed with a RED BORDER.

829 Extra cloth, beveled, red edges............... $1 25
2847 Turkey mor., ant. extra, gilt edges............. 4 00
2851 "   "   circuit, gilt edges............... 5 00
2855 Calf, flexible, gilt edges....................... 4 50

The Imitation of Christ.
32mo edition, 481 pages

2726 Cloth... $0 50
2729 Extra cloth, beveled, red edges................   65
2736 French mor., gilt centre and edges............. 1 00
2747 Turkey mor., ant. extra, gilt edges............ 2 50
2753 Calf, ant., red edges.......................... 2 75
2755 "   flexible, gilt edges....................... 2 75

Manual of the Sodality
of the Blessed Virgin Mary.

Containing the Rules, Privileges, Indulgences, and exercises of Piety suitable for all Christians.
32mo, 613 pages.

1926 Cloth... $0 50
1929 "   extra, beveled, red edges..................   75
1937 French mor., full gilt sides, back, and edges.... 1 25
1947 Turkey mor., extra ant., gilt centre and edges.. 2 50
1948 "   "   super, full gilt sides, back, and edg. 2 50
1956 Calf, flexible, red edges....................... 2 75

BENZIGER BROTHERS, New York, Cincinnati, and St. Louis.

NEW PUBLICATIONS.

The Monk's Pardon.

*A Historical Romance of the time of
Philip IV. of Spain.*

Translated from the French of RAOUL DE NAVÉRY

By ANNA T. SADLIER

12mo, cloth, $1.25.

—o—

This is one of the best works of perhaps the most popular Catholic novelist of France. The plot is strictly historical, the style pure, the interest admirably sustained and the moral excellent. It needs only to be known to acquire the popularity of the original, which has run through many editions in France.

Natalie Narischkin,

Sister of Charity of St. Vincent of Paul.

Translated from the French of **Mme. AUGUSTUS CRAVEN,**

By Lady GEORGIANA FULLERTON.

12mo, cloth, $1.00.

This book by the author of "A Sister's Story" is the biography of a noble Russian girl who becoming a Catholic, joined the Sisters of Charity, and devoted her life to working and suffering, as one Saint among a thousand others, in an institute where heroism is as common as the ordinary virtues are elsewhere, and sanctity is the universal rule. The narrative, enriched with copious extracts from her letters and numerous personal anecdotes, is interesting and edifying.

BENZIGER BROTHERS, New York, Cincinnati, and St. Louis.

My First Communion:
The Happiest Day of My Life.

A Preparation and Remembrance for First Communicants. Translated from the German of Rev. J. N. BUCHMANN, O.S.B., *by* Rev. RICHARD BRENNAN, LL.D.

With a Chromo-Frontispiece, and many full-page and other Illustrations. Extra cloth, 75 cents.

APPROBATIONS.

From the Right Rev. Bishop of Louisville.
"* * * It is a charming work, one of the best of its kind."

From Right Rev. Bishop of Erie.
"* * * Admirably calculated both in its style and the character of its contents to interest and instruct those for whom it is intended, the work should, and I hope will, receive a cordial welcome from parents, teachers, pastors, in fine all engaged in the training of youth."

From Right Rev. Bishop of Buffalo.
"* * * I believe that this 'delightfully interesting little volume will be welcomed *not only* by the children,' but by all good Pastors as well, to whom the first Communion of their children is one of the happiest and most important events of their holy ministry."

From Right Rev. Bishop of Providence.
"* * * I know no other book treating of the Most Holy Communion so well adapted to prepare children for that Sacrament and to leave wholesome, lasting impressions on their minds."

From Right Rev. Bishop of Ogdensburg.
"Your excellent book 'My First Communion,' I read with interest and edification."

From Right Rev. Bishop of Monterey and Los Angeles.
"* * * I heartily approve it and recommend it to our flock and Pastors."

From Right Rev. Vicar-Apostolic of Northern Minnesota.
"May this little book find a large circulation, and assist many to fervent and frequent Communions."

BENZIGER BROTHERS, New York, Cincinnati, and St. Louis.

A LETTER FROM
His Holiness Pope Leo XIII.

Sacrorum Bibliorum volumen et obsequii sensus, quos per Episcopum Basiliensem fratres Benziger editores Nobis obtulerunt, grato animo excepimus; eosque et eorum operam, ut religioni semper bene vertat, Apostolica Benedictione prosequimur.

                          LEO P. P. XIII.

(Translation.)

We have received with thanks the copy of The Bible History, together with the expressions of devotion, which **Benziger Brothers**, publishers, have sent us through the Bishop of Basel, and we give our Apostolic Benediction to them and to their labors, that these may always tend to the good of Religion.

                          LEO P. P. XIII.

BIBLE HISTORY, 140 Illustrations, 60 cents.

GREETINGS
TO THE
CHRIST-CHILD.

A Collection of Christmas Poems for the Young.

EMBELLISHED WITH 89 ILLUSTRATIONS, TAILPIECES, ETC., ETC.

Square 16mo, on fine, super-calendered, tinted paper, full gilt back and gilt edges, elegant side stamp in gold, 50c.

BENZIGER BROTHERS, New York, Cincinnati, and St. Louis.

THE LIFE OF
OUR LORD AND SAVIOUR JESUS CHRIST
AND OF HIS BLESSED MOTHER.

Translated and adapted from the original of Rev. L. C. BUSINGER,

By Rev. RICHARD BRENNAN, LL.D.,

Author of "A Popular Life of Pope Pius IX."

This is the first fully illustrated work on this subject ever published. It has nearly 600 Engravings in the body of the text, Chromo-Lithographs and Fine Plates; together with a superb Steel Engraving of "The Resurrection of Our Lord" (Size 20½x27 inches), which is

PRESENTED FREE

to every subscriber. The book is issued in 38 parts at

25 CENTS EACH,

and sold only by subscription.

BENZIGER BROTHERS, New York, Cincinnati, and St. Louis.

www.ingramcontent.com/pod-product-compliance
Lightning Source LLC
Chambersburg PA
CBHW032118230426
43672CB00009B/1777